W9-AFH-458

Introduction:
The Power of Pretend Play

Children love to pretend! Role playing or pretending to be another person or an animal or a creature, are all activities that children engage in naturally, with little or no encouragement from adults. As part of these activities, children often create their own costumes and "wardrobes" from whatever materials are available: a stick becomes a sword or a wand, a rock becomes a hammer or a treasure, and a scarf becomes a cape or a skirt. Providing costumes and dress-up props can help make imaginary play more meaningful and fun. These items reinforce the importance of such play and add new possibilities to any pretend scenario. Providing props can also stretch pretend play and enhance learning in many areas.

From *Nifty, Thrifty, No-Sew Costumes & Props* published by Good Year

Learning Areas

MATH AND NUMBERS: Measuring devices, money and cash registers, price tags or signs, telephones, and watches and clocks are examples of props that promote the recognition and use of numbers.

SCIENCE: Magnifying glasses, thermometers, magnets, flashlights, and the wide variety of other props that suggest such occupations as astronaut, doctor, firefighter, and farmer present many opportunities for children to explore and experience science.

LANGUAGE AND LITERACY: Props such as books and other reading materials, writing instruments, and signs and labels greatly enhance literacy. And, as children interact with each other and communicate through speech, their language skills are strengthened. It is during these informal pretend play settings that children "try out" language that they may hear in real life or in books that are read to them. They experiment with language, using improvisational dialogue and communicating in different ways.

SOCIAL STUDIES AND CULTURAL AWARENESS: Props and costumes associated with a variety of regions and occupations give children an opportunity to experience, understand, and appreciate diversity in people and cultures.

ART, MUSIC, AND MOVEMENT: As children create signs and help make props, they engage in a variety of art activities. In addition, any costume, real or imaginary, invokes a range of movement and motion that, with or without music, promotes the development of motor skills.

Use in the Classroom and Home

Use costumes, dress-up clothes, accessories, and props in any Dramatic Play corner in the classroom or with any toys in the home. Consider adding costumes and dress-up props to other areas of the classroom or home as well, including: the block or building area, the library or book corner, the music area, and even the playground or backyard area. If full costumes are impractical for these areas, incorporate a basket or box of hats, jewelry, or props for children to use if they choose. Move the items back to the Dramatic Play corner or costume box at the end of play so that items remain an occasional feature of the area rather than a permanent fixture. Remember, dress-up clothes and props in an area not usually associated with such materials can take play in that area in exciting new directions.

Pretend Play Every Day

Incorporate costuming and props into the day on a regular basis. Many early childhood activities lend themselves especially well to the inclusion of costumes and props—language activities, story times, music, games, birthday parties, and group times, among them. The inclusion of costumes and related props in rou-

From *Nifty, Thrifty, No-Sew Costumes & Props* published by Good Year Books. Copyright © 1998 Good Year Books.

Nifty, Thrifty, No-Sew

Costumes & Props

Carol Ann Bloom

Good Year Books

An Imprint of Addison-Wesley Educational Publishers, Inc.

This book is dedicated to:

My grandmother, Cora Chamberlain, for my very first handmade costumes.

My parents, Richard and Norma Bloom, for their love and encouragement.

And my sister, Sherry, who is my favorite person to dress up with!

Acknowledgments:

It is with much appreciation that I thank and acknowledge the following people—

Sherry J. Bloom for countless behind-the-scenes tasks: from helping to choose materials and make costumes to offering ideas and proofreading directions.

Aleene's®, Delta®, and Plaid® for providing their fine craft products.

Roberta Dempsey for her initial interest in this project.

Laura Strom for her friendship, support, and expertise in assemblying this book.

Nancy Rudd for a wonderful book design and artwork.

The Scott Foresman - Addison Wesley photo studio for the fun and lively photography.

And Aaron Adams-Harvey, Cody Cromwell, Elijahben Israel, Zak Johnson, Gabriella Martinez, Sarah Mounger, Bobby Ortiz, Paige Pignaz, Rita Semro, Jennifer Strom, and Blake Willis for bringing each costume to life with their enthusiasm and imagination.

· ·

Good Year Books are available for most basic curriculum subjects plus many enrichment areas. For more Good Year Books, contact your local bookseller or educational dealer. For a complete catalog with information about other Good Year Books, please write:

Good Year Books
1900 East Lake Avenue
Glenview, IL 60025

Table of Contents

tine activities adds a sense of excitement to the day. It also gives children opportunities to take on new roles. Frequently, children who are reluctant participants in activities join in more readily when costumes, hats, and props are involved.

Planning Special Events

Plan events that will make use of costumes and props. Choose from the existing dress-up supply or create a group of costumes specifically for the event. Use full costumes or just a group of hats and related props. Vary the participants during events, so that all children have a turn on the same day or on subsequent days. If possible, plan an activity in which an entire group has an opportunity to wear costumes or dress-up accessories and/or use props. The easy-to-make and interchangeable costumes in this book (tunics, collars, vests, capes, hats, and much more) provide the potential for a large dress-up supply from which to choose. Try dress-up accessories and costumes for reenactments of familiar tales and books, multiple-verse songs, children's plays, collections of verses, child-written stories, holiday celebrations, and field trips.

Idea Starters

For more easy and fun ideas for expanding your use of costumes, consult the "Idea Starters" features sprinkled throughout this book.

The Benefits of Pretend Play

EXERCISE IMAGINATION AND CREATIVITY: Pretending and imagining give children an opportunity to explore their feelings about and perceptions of the world. Thus they serve as an important outlet for children, one that most children discover quite naturally on their own. The addition of costumes, dress-up clothes, and props encourages and stimulates children to become even more involved in their pretend play. They clarify their perceptions of the world and exchange ideas with others. There is particular value in pretend play when it is presented in a group setting or with friends. Children serve as audiences for one another, helping each other more fully realize and enjoy the power of their own imagination and creativity. The pleasure and benefit children derive from these play experiences are unparalleled in any other activity and can be extremely rewarding. Indeed, a child who thinks creatively can look at problems and situations from more than one viewpoint. He or she learns to solve problems in a variety of ways, rather than fix on one "right" solution. This is a skill that can be very helpful in later schooling and general life situations.

PRACTICE A VARIETY OF LITERACY (EARLY READING AND WRITING) SKILLS: Many children are apt to make more realistic use of props, both real and imaginary, when dressed in costumes and other accessories. Whether using a stick to "write" out a speeding ticket or making a grocery list with a pencil and paper, imitating adult behaviors during pretend play allows children to practice literacy skills long before they engage in conventional reading and writing. In imitating literacy behaviors in these self-initiated play settings, children have countless opportunities to recognize the many applications of letters and numbers in daily life. In so doing, children experience feelings of success and accomplishment that cannot be duplicated in any other setting. The comfort and familiarity that they gain from using the many tools of literacy in the natural course of play contributes to a solid foundation for later experiences with literacy.

BUILD AND ENRICH LANGUAGE SKILLS: Communication is a natural part of any pretend play setting that involves two or more children. As children interact and converse with one another, they practice language skills and react to the language of others. In order to "play" and act out roles, children frequently must talk with each other and, more importantly, clarify their ideas. Vocabulary is strengthened, self-expression is enhanced, and listening skills are practiced when children strive to both understand and be understood by others. During pretend play children also have many opportunities to "try out" language they hear elsewhere (real-life situations, television, films, and books read to them). Such experimenting with language allows children to step beyond their usual communication patterns and try something new.

ENHANCE UNDERSTANDING OF THE ENVIRONMENT: Young children are continually experiencing something new in their environments. A trip to the bakery, an afternoon at the zoo, a meal at a restaurant, or an overnight stay with a friend are just a few examples of the daily interactions children have with their environment. Assimilating new experiences is one way children learn about the world and their place in it. When they re-create these experiences through role play and the use of props, children extend their understanding of their environment; that is, they make more sense out of their "worldly" experiences when they have an opportunity to act them out.

CROSS THE BARRIERS OF GENDER STEREOTYPING: In pretend play all things are possible. It is this element of freedom that allows children to be people, animals, birds, dinosaurs, or even aliens and monsters. Just as children can be anything they can imagine, they can also take on any role and perform any action or activity related to that role. Thus there exists in imaginary play countless opportunities for children to cross traditional gender stereotypes. The inhibitions of gender stereotyping found in many other types of play can be virtually nonexistent here. Girls CAN fight fires, fix cars, own the store, pilot the airplane, pump the gas, or be the doctor. Boys CAN do the shopping, run the vacuum, do the laundry, cook the dinner, and care for babies. Gender equality in pretend play is as limitless as the interests and imaginations of the children who engage in such play. Costumes, dress-up clothes, and props extend this freedom as children move in and out of various role-play settings.

From *Nifty, Thrifty, No-Sew Costumes & Props* published by Good Year Books. Copyright © 1998 Good Year Books.

HAVE POSITIVE INTERACTIONS WITH PEERS: Unlike many forms of play in which young children often play next to, but not really with, one another, dress-up play almost always encourages true interaction. And, since this form of play is so enjoyable and satisfying for children, these interactions tend to be very positive. Through role play and reenactment, children's interactions are influenced by the people and creatures they pretend to be. As they interact and react to their own roles and those of their peers, they are apt to show more patience, kindness, and understanding. The more young children learn about others in a positive atmosphere, the more they will understand and appreciate differences in themselves and their friends. In dress-up play, children have the opportunity to share their cultural and family traditions and to learn about those of others. Props and dress-up clothes should ALWAYS reflect the cultures and backgrounds of the children that participate in the play. If you are a teacher, make certain that customs and traditions are accurately represented by asking parents for suggestions for dress-up pieces and involving them in the collection of props.

PRACTICE NEGOTIATION AND PROBLEM-SOLVING SKILLS: When children choose roles and set the stage for pretend play, they engage in conversation, discussion, and negotiation. During the course of dress-up play, children confront numerous situations in which conflicts may arise and must be resolved. To settle disputes between themselves or the characters they play, children must converse, negotiate, and eventually arrive at an acceptable solution. Learning to get along, compromise, control anger, and

resolve conflicts will be essential to any successful and sustained pretend scenario. Problem-solving skills and sensitivity to the needs of others are enhanced as children, either independently or with the gentle help and support of adults, proceed in these spontaneous play settings.

LEARN TO SHARE AND TAKE TURNS: There are countless opportunities for children to practice turn-taking and sharing when using the dress-up clothes and props that accompany imaginary play. As they help each other with costumes and trade props, for example, children learn patience and cooperation. When sharing and turn-taking goals are successfully met, children gain firsthand knowledge of the benefits of compromise and the rewards of patience. This can be an important and gratifying learning experience, one that may well carry over to other nonplay situations and have a lasting effect.

EXPERIENCE AND LEARN TO UNDERSTAND A VARIETY OF FEELINGS AND EMOTIONS: Any pretend play scenario can present opportunities for young children to encounter a range of emotions: the excitement of putting out a fire in the role of a firefighter, the anxiety of performing as a ballerina, the concern for a sick baby doll or stuffed animal, and the fear associated with visiting a pretend doctor or dentist. Learning to work through a range of emotions and take into account the feelings of others is essential for the healthy development of the whole child.

COPE WITH STRESS: There are many new situations in a young child's life that arouse anxiety and even fear: a visit to the doctor or dentist, a trip to the hospital, a first day at school, the birth of a new sibling, a new baby-sitter, and a performance in front of an audience. All are examples of stressful situations that young children may encounter. Reenacting these experiences in a pretend play setting helps children understand and overcome their fears. For example, seeing a peer in the role of a doctor, dentist, or baby-sitter or reenacting the role themselves can produce very positive results. Children's realization that they are not alone and that other children experience the same fears and anxieties that they do helps to alleviate concerns.

MAKE CHOICES AND SELF-DIRECT: In dress-up play, children often set the scenario, choose roles, and decide which costumes and props to use. In a world in which many decisions are made for them, pretend play offers children the much-needed opportunity to exercise their own will and make their own choices. In the process, assertiveness, independence, and good judgment are strengthened.

TRY OUT NEW SKILLS: Children love to try new things, use new tools, and do something that they have never done before. When adult gadgets and tools are added to the mix, children's fascination with the new and unusual increases. Imitating parents, people they see in the community, storybook characters, and other adults is one of the pleasures of childhood. As children role-play, they become involved in new adventures with each new play scenario. They excitedly try new things that they might not even find interesting in other situations. In so doing, children develop new skills and strengthen emerging abilities.

IMPROVE MOTOR SKILLS: Movement is an important part of pretend play. All parts of the body are exercised as children walk, climb, jump, crawl, drive, cook, serve, bake, plant, fix, examine, dance, snarl, and growl. The addition of props to play provides more opportunities for children to hone coordination and develop motor skills. Using tools, pressing buttons, turning knobs and keys, writing, typing, and stirring are but a few of the many actions that children may perform. Gross and fine motor skills are strengthened as children use their muscles, large and small, in imaginary play. Even the preparation for play requires manual dexterity, as children dress and use fasteners, laces, hats, shoes, and jewelry.

STRENGTHEN COGNITIVE SKILLS: When children engage in pretend play and exercise their imaginations, they become more flexible thinkers. As they set up and enact imaginary play plots, for example, they develop the ability to sequence events and follow story lines. During role play, children also make many choices about what adults might do and say, increasing their knowledge base and cognitive skills. Imaginary play often involves substituting one object for another and using something abstract to represent, or symbolize, something concrete. In later reading, writing, and number work, children will learn to do the same thing—use letters, words, and numbers to symbolize concepts. Early, informal, and enjoyable experiences with symbolic play serve as a valuable foundation and a natural bridge to later learning.

From *Nifty, Thrifty, No-Sew Costumes & Props* published by Good Year Books. Copyright © 1998 Good Year Books.

BUILD SELF-ESTEEM AND SELF-CONFIDENCE:
Many aspects of dress-up play help young children build self-esteem and strengthen self-confidence. When children make their own choices in pretend play, they become more confident decision-makers in other areas of their lives as well. As children build positive relationships with other children, self-esteem grows. There is nothing as satisfying as having ideas and thoughts accepted by others. Dress-up play provides children with many opportunities to offer opinions, set forth plans, and enact roles in ways that will be accepted and appreciated by others. As the play proceeds, children become more capable and confident in their actions, increasing the likelihood of comfortable future peer interactions. Even children who are quite reserved often shed their inhibitions when given the opportunity to wear a costume. In these and other ways, pretend play situations contribute to a positive self-image that can favorably affect the child's future activities.

EXPERIENCE A SENSE OF SATISFACTION AND PLEASURE: In pretend play there are few right or wrong answers and little risk of failure. What pretend play does offer is numerous opportunities to set goals, experience success, and recognize accomplishments. Children learn to feel good about themselves and what they are doing. At times the reenactments and role play become so involved that children get completely immersed in the play. As they "become" the role, character, or creature, children experience immense pleasure and satisfaction. This joy is one of the most, if not the most, important benefits of pretend play: it IS the real power of pretend play.

Play that occurs so naturally and enhances so many areas of early development should be part of every child's life. For you, it is as easy as providing the costumes, dress-up clothes, and props presented on the following pages and giving children the freedom to take off on wings of imagination.

EDITOR'S NOTE: All measurements are in the U.S. Customary system. To convert to metric, use the chart below:

inches x 2.54 = centimeters

feet x .3048 = meters

ounces x 29.57 = milliliters

ounces x .03 = liters

1 cup = 8 oz. = 237ml = .24l

1 tablespoon = $\frac{1}{2}$ oz. = 14.8ml

1 teaspoon = $\frac{1}{3}$ tablespoon = 4.9ml

Making Costumes: Getting Started

Building a Costume Collection

A costume collection is an invaluable classroom resource as well as a wonderful addition for home instruction, group activities, or general play. In addition to its obvious importance in a dramatic play area, a costume wardrobe will come in handy for use in many other areas of the classroom, curriculum, and home. Begin with a few collected and constructed pieces and build on the collection, adding to it as the need arises for new characters and creatures. Storing the collection and changing or adding pieces to the collection as needed will keep costumes and pretend play fresh and spontaneous.

The Tunics, Collars, Capes, and other basic pieces in Chapter 2 are the foundation of the costume collection. It is with these interchangeable, multi-functional pieces that a limitless variety of characters can be created. The accessory pieces (Chapters 3–6) and the props, both wearable and portable (Chapters 7 and 8), are added to the basic pieces to individualize and differentiate characters and creatures, making the collection come alive. Chapter 9 offers money-saving recipes for making your own materials. Chapter 10 includes reproducible patterns for making costumes. Chapter 11 is a Full-Color Costume and Prop Reference Guide (pp. 174-190), which highlights 32 different costumes, and will help you choose and locate the props and accessories necessary to complete each character. Within the book you will notice variations on costumes so you can get more from your pieces. Let your imagination and the interests of the children determine other characters to create on the foundation of the basic costume pieces.

Adult clothing placed in a dress-up area, although appealing to children, is often not the best choice for dress-up play for a number of reasons:

- small trims and buttons are a safety hazard

- ill-fitting clothing can be too warm or otherwise uncomfortable

- overly long clothing is a safety hazard; in particular, long ties, sashes, and belts can get caught or tripped over

- children have more difficulty dressing themselves in adult clothing and often require adult assistance; this limits independence and stifles spontaneous play

- pieces often differ widely, which may cause quarrels over favorites and problems with sharing and turn-taking

Constructing costumes and costume accessories for young children enables teachers and parents to tailor dress-up clothing to the size and developmental stage of the majority of children in the classroom or group, or the child or children at home. Keep these considerations in mind when constructing costumes and dress-up clothing for children's use and enjoyment.

SAFETY: Costumes should not include very small pieces or trims that are loosely fastened. Costumes for very young children should not include small pieces at all. Avoid costumes that are so long that they drag on the floor. Most of the dress-up clothing in this book can be constructed so that it does not hang below the knee. Apparel for legs and feet should be discrete pieces, separate from the basic costume. Additions to costumes, such as tails, wings, and feathers, should be large enough to be fun but not so large that they get in the way of play. In general, children should wear shoes in pretend play areas, particularly if floors are not carpeted. To accessories that fit over shoes and lower legs, attach a tie or stirrup so that the majority of the sole of the shoe maintains contact with the floor. Make socks or felt coverings skid-proof by applying several lines of rubber cement directly to the sock or felt sole. After sufficient drying time, the rubber cement creates just enough traction so that feet will not slip on bare floors. Coverings on the head should not extend onto the face or obscure vision (full face masks are not included in this resource for obvious safety reasons and because many children find them frightening or intimidating.) The age and size of the children using the costumes and the space available for play are the best guides for constructing costumes that are both safe and comfortable.

COMFORT: Next to safety, comfort is the most important consideration. If children do not feel comfortable in dress-up clothing, they are less likely to use it; and if they do use it, they are less likely to enjoy the experience. Since costumes are usually worn over clothing, they should not be too cumbersome or heavy. Ideally, costumes should cover the chest area only, accompanied by additional pieces, such as leg or arm coverings, that can be worn separately. The best model for any dress-up costume is a tunic or vest piece, as described in Chapter 2 of this resource. The basic tunic costume hangs loosely from the shoulders and has no arms or legs. Such costumes offer children complete freedom of movement and enhance opportunities for long periods of sustained play. Lacking sleeves and covering the top portion of the body only, they fit comfortably over any kind of clothing. Similarly, accessory pieces that cover only the tops of the hands and feet, and fasten with ties, elastic, or Velcro, are much less awkward than full-piece costumes and provide for better manual dexterity and greater freedom of movement.

EASE OF USE: Be sure costumes and dress-up pieces are easy for children to put on themselves. This promotes independence and self-sufficiency. It also expedites the process of symbolic play, making it more spontaneous. When children have to wait for an adult's help or for a friend's assistance, spontaneity and immediacy of play suffers. Tunics and vests, and other basic costumes slip over the head and need no fasteners. Children, especially younger ones, may, however, require some help with fasteners on hats, capes, or hand and foot coverings. Often, children can assist each other with elastic, laces, or Velcro fasteners. All costumes and accessory pieces presented in this resource are one-size-fits-all, eliminating the need to search through clothing for the right fit or wear ill-fitting clothing.

EASE OF CONSTRUCTION: Sewing is NOT required for any of the costumes, dress-up pieces, accessories, or props in this resource. Available in a wide range of colors and inexpensive, felt is the material of choice for many of the costumes. In addition, felt is a durable fabric that stands up to frequent and multiple wearings. This user-friendly fabric cuts easily with scissors or pinking shears and will not fray or ravel. Since the costumes are one-size-fits-all, the same measurements work for many different costume styles. It's easy to alter the dimensions, simply adjust the suggested length several inches longer or shorter.

Idea Starter

COSTUMES AND PARTIES: Don't limit costume wearing to Halloween or dress-up play! Incorporate costumes into a theme party, a sleepover, or any special celebration. Provide each child with a costume that relates to the party theme, decorate the party area, and provide each guest with a special party favor. At an Elf or Fairy (pp. 181, 182) Party, give each child a wand (p. 134) favor; at an Outer Space Party, give each Astronaut (p. 175) a pouch (p. 123) of moon rocks; or at a Cat Party, give each Cat (p. 177) a collar (p. 100) with a bell attached. Each child can also construct their own favor at the party as a play activity.

From *Nifty, Thrifty, No-Sew Costumes & Props* published by Good Year Books. Copyright © 1998 Good Year Books.

Before You Start

MATERIALS AND SPACE CONSIDERATIONS: Availability of materials and limited storage space are familiar problems in both the home and early childhood classroom. The tunics and other costume pieces suggested in the next chapter provide the perfect solution. Not only do they store flat and require little space, but, with slight alterations, each can be used to depict a range of people, animals, and other dress-ups favorites. For example, a basic blue tunic forms the base for a police officer (add a badge and a name tag), a mail carrier (add a flag or a USPS patch), a fairy (add wings and a jeweled necklace), and even a bird (with the addition of feathers). Make attachments permanent by gluing them on, or temporary by using Velcro, tape, or semi-permanent glue. The props and accessory pieces add the finishing touches: hats, a steering wheel, a mail bag, a wand, or a beak.

INVOLVING CHILDREN: Children can help construct many of the costumes—either from start to finish or at the decorating stage. Viewed as a goal-oriented project, costume making gives children an opportunity to take part in creating items that they will later put to use in play. Children will better understand the purpose of the dress-up materials and be more motivated to try them when they help to make and/or decorate them. Excitement and anticipation build as children engage in the activity and prepare to use the finished items.

Precut and prepare larger pieces in advance, assemble the necessary tools and materials, then engage children in any of the following preparations:

- glue on spots, stripes, and other paper or felt features
- use acrylic or dimensional paints, to add features and decorations
- lace yarn ties and attachments
- mix clays for jewelry beads
- weave yarn or ribbon on baskets and tote bag props
- apply wet strips on papier-mâché projects
- cut polystyrene foam pieces for claws, jewelry, and various props
- wrap props and accessories with foil
- wind starched yarn around objects to make curls for wigs
- stuff legs from tights and sleeves from shirts, for hats and tails
- trace their own hands, for making antlers
- wrap yarn for making tassels and pom-poms
- string beads and pasta for jewelry
- cover buttons with glitter, for jewelry and other decoration
- make tissue-paper flowers
- help mix art recipes

Materials Needed

Many of the materials needed to make the costumes and props in this resource are easy-to-find recyclables. Durable enough to withstand the rigors of play and multiple uses, they are also easily repaired or replaced. Be inventive when collecting materials, and substitute those that are more readily available for those that are more difficult to find. Many common classroom or household supplies come in handy for costume and prop construction. Other (optional) supplies that are less likely to be found in the classroom or home can be purchased in most craft stores or in craft departments. Such supplies are generally easy to find and quite affordable. Remember, craft supplies can be used for more than one costume or prop—a little goes a long way. Unique craft supplies add a finished quality to costumes and make them so appealing to children that such products are well worth using. Several companies; such as Plaid®, Delta®, and Aleene's®; make terrific products in these categories. Check with your local craft store for a recommendation.

A good pair of scissors and a utility knife are needed for many of the projects. A basic materials list is provided before each set of costume instructions. Be sure to read the instructions all the way through and decide on your method of decoration before finalizing your materials list.

Following are general lists of some of the materials you will want to have on hand to make the dress-up pieces described in this resource. Specific materials needed for each piece are given throughout this book.

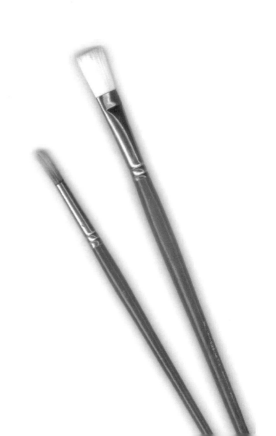

From *Nifty, Thrifty, No-Sew Costumes & Props* published by Good Year Books. Copyright © 1998 Good Year Books.

Idea Starter

COSTUMES AND STORY TIME: Use a selection of costumes (or just hats) to re-enact a favorite story or book. As the story is read, the child wearing the speaking character's related costume (or hat) can stand, perform a motion, or speak a story line. As the story becomes familiar, children will enjoy retelling it themselves in costume.

Materials List

Costume Materials

- adult T-shirts
- brown paper grocery bags
- bubble wrap
- felt
- pillowcases
- poster board or lightweight cardboard
- scarves
- tulle or netting

Assembly Materials

- adhesive bandages
- balloons
- brass fasteners
- chenille stems (pipe cleaners)
- double-stick tape
- elastic (round cord)
- glues (white craft, tacky, temporary, Stitchless®, Mod Podge®, washable—depending on your needs)
- hole punch
- liquid starch
- markers, pencils
- masking tape
- paper clips
- pinking sheers
- rubber bands
- rubber cement
- scissors
- spring clothespins
- staples (if used, place the staple so that the smooth side faces the skin and tape over rough edges if necessary)
- tape measure
- Velcro® (self-stick dots or tape)

Accessory and Prop Materials

- aluminum foil
- brown paper grocery bags
- buttons
- cellophane
- clothesline
- construction paper

- corrugated cardboard
- cotton
- crepe paper
- egg cartons
- fabric scraps
- felt
- gift wrap and gift wrap tubes (cardboard)
- gloves and mittens
- greeting cards
- magazine pictures
- newspaper
- old belts
- paper plates and cups
- paper twist
- pasta
- plastic berry baskets
- plastic garbage bags
- plastic headbands
- plastic lids (from margarine containers, coffee cans, and frozen juice cans)
- plastic liter soda bottles and plastic water or milk jugs
- polystyrene foam balls, food trays, egg cartons
- poster board or lightweight cardboard (gift box cardboard works well)
- ribbon
- shoe boxes
- six-pack plastic rings
- sleeves from old sweatshirts
- small paper bags
- socks
- string
- stuffing materials (cotton, shredded paper, fiberfill)
- tights or opaque stockings (old or worn)
- tissue paper
- trash bag fasteners and twist ties
- tree branches (small)
- wallpaper
- yarn

Decoration Materials

(*Some of these items can be made by following the instructions provided in this resource.)

- artificial flowers*
- beads*
- bells
- bottle caps
- bows*
- buttons
- chenelle stems (pipe cleaners)
- colored tape
- crepe paper
- corks
- cotton
- decorative snow
- Delta® Dazzlers: Liquid Stars, Liquid Confetti
- doilies (paper)
- feathers*
- felt scraps
- glitter
- holiday tinsel
- Mylar and foil papers
- novelty charms
- paint (acrylic, fabric, dimensional, tempera, metallic, glitter, pearl, highlighter)
- permanent markers
- plastic gems
- polystyrene foam (balls, cones, and sheets)
- pompoms
- ribbon
- sealers and varnishes (water based)
- sequins
- stencils
- stickers, foil stars
- straw
- string
- tassels*
- wiggle eyes
- wooden beads
- yarn

Caution: Some items on this list could be dangerous and a choking hazard for small children. Use caution when using these materials around them.

Costume Basics:
Characters You Can Be, Real and Imaginary

The basic costume style presented in this chapter is the tunic. With just a few simple adjustments to the Basic Tunic pattern, you can make many other items, such as collars, vests, and capes. Also provided in this chapter are easy-to-follow instructions for constructing skirts, pillowcase costumes, and T-shirt costumes. Additionally, you'll find suggestions for embellishing the costumes with a variety of trims and accessories.

Patterns are provided for Tunics, Collars, Vests, and Capes on pp. 147–165.

1 **Basic Tunics**

Cut **Neck Opening**　Fold	Cut **Neck Opening**　Fold	Cut **Neck Opening**　Fold	Cut **Neck Opening**　Fold
V-Shaped	**Straight Cut**	**Rounded**	**Jagged**
Cut **Neck Opening**　Fold	Cut **Neck Opening**　Fold	Cut **Neck Opening**　Fold	Cut **Neck Opening**　Fold
Scalloped	**Squared**	**Fringed**	**Wavy**

The Basic Tunic (DRAWING 1)

Make tunics in a variety of colors. One yard of 36" or 52" wide felt will make several tunics. Save excess felt for accessory pieces, such as hats, shoes, paws, or tails, and decorative pieces, such as flowers, spots, and stripes. *(SEE PATTERNS pp. 147-153.)*

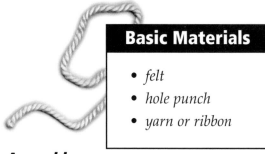

Basic Materials

- *felt*
- *hole punch*
- *yarn or ribbon*

Assembly:

1. Cut a rectangular piece of felt 12"–16" × 32"–40". (Choose the dimensions that best suit your needs or construct costumes in the full range of sizes so as to accommodate a variety of children.)

2. Fold the piece in half, making a 12"–16" × 16"–20". Cut a neck hole opening in the folded side. Leave 2"–3" of felt on either side of the opening to lay across the shoulders *(SEE DRAWING 1).*

3. Cut a 6" slit from the center of the opening straight down the back. This lets children slip the tunic over their heads more easily.

4. Leave tunic as is, or place a fastener on either side of the slit. (Since felt adheres well to other fabrics, fasteners are not necessary.) To fasten, attach a self-stick Velcro dot on both sides of the opening. Or, punch a hole on each side and thread a piece of yarn or ribbon through the holes to tie closed. *Note:* The front and the back of the tunic will look the same except for the slit and fasteners, which will be in the back.

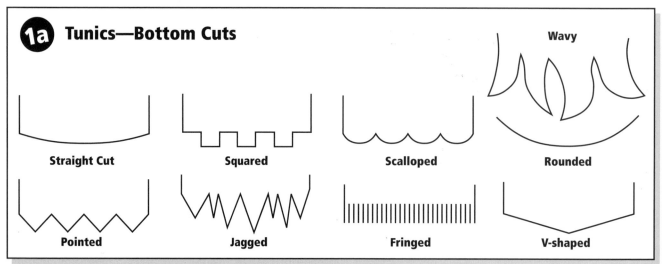

1a Tunics—Bottom Cuts

Straight Cut **Squared** **Scalloped** **Rounded**

Wavy

Pointed **Jagged** **Fringed** **V-shaped**

From *Nifty, Thrifty, No-Sew Costumes & Props* published by Good Year Books. Copyright © 1998 Good Year Books.

1b **Tunics—Shoulder Cuts**

(overhead view)   **(front view)**

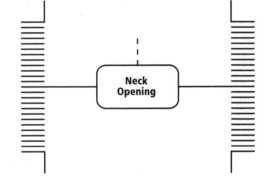

Neck Opening

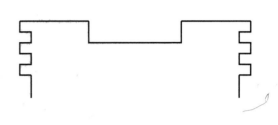

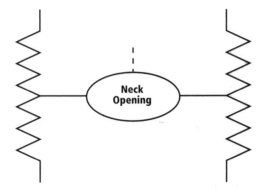

Neck Opening

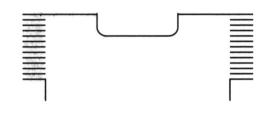

Neck Opening

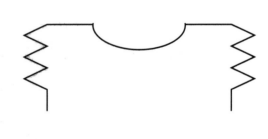

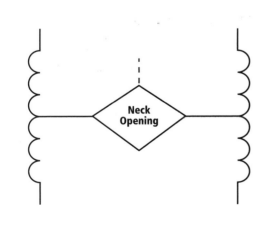

Neck Opening

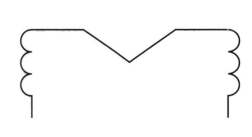

5. Cut the bottom edge of the tunic straight across or make a decorative cut *(SEE DRAWING 1A)*. Correlate the cut to the character or animal being depicted. A decorative edging can also be cut on the shoulder area, where the tunic will meet the upper arms *(SEE DRAWING 1B)*. Cuts should extend 4"–6" down on either side. Attach decorations permanently or temporarily to suggest a variety of characters and animals.

Animal Tunics *(DRAWING 2)*

This felt tunic is constructed following the same procedure as the Basic Tunic, with the addition of a tail extending from the back panel. *(SEE PATTERNS P. 154.)*

Basic Materials

- *felt*
- *hole punch*
- *yarn or ribbon*
- *chenille stems*
- *fabric glue*

Assembly:

1. Cut a rectangular piece of felt 12"–16" × 40"–45".

2. Fold the piece in half, making a 12"–16" × 15" rectangle in the front and a 12"–16" × 25"–30" rectangle in the back. Cut a neck hole as described in step 2 of the Basic Tunic (p. 18).

3. Cut a 6" slit as described in step 3 of the Basic Tunic.

4. Attach fasteners as needed *(SEE BASIC TUNIC)*.

5. Select bottom cuts and shoulder cuts as appropriate *(SEE BASIC TUNIC)*.

6. To form the tail, start at the fold and measure down 15"; this is where the tail will begin. Make two (horizontal) cuts into both sides of the felt, each 3"–4" in length *(SEE DRAWING 2)*.

7. Cut the tail shape *(SEE DRAWING 2)*, making it 4"–6" wide and 10"–15" long. Adjust the length of the tail to suit the size of the children who will wear the costumes. Longer tails can be curled and bent with the addi-

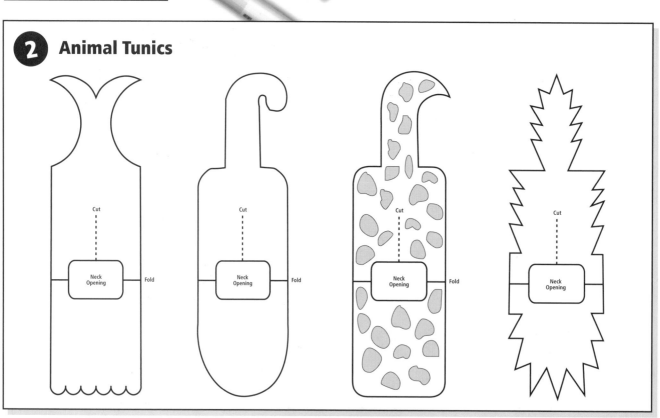

2 **Animal Tunics**

Cut · Neck Opening · Fold
Cut · Neck Opening · Fold
Cut · Neck Opening · Fold
Cut · Neck Opening

From *Nifty, Thrifty, No-Sew Costumes & Props* published by Good Year Books. Copyright © 1998 Good Year Books.

3 Collars

(overhead view)

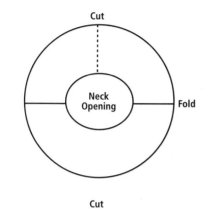

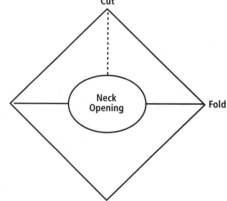

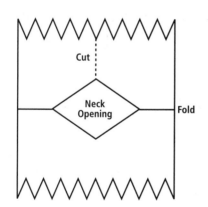

(front view)

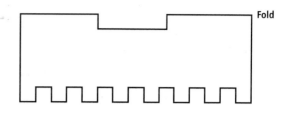

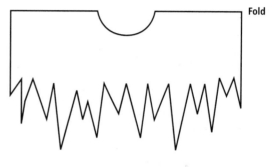

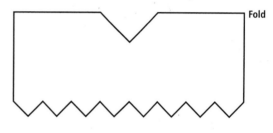

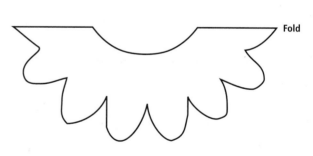

Shirt Collars

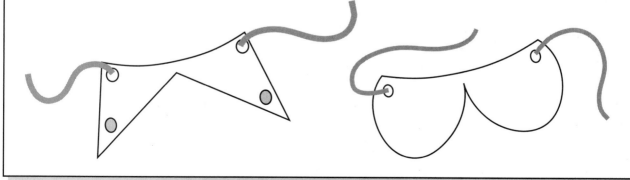

tion of chenille stems. Attach chenille stems to the middle of the underside of the tails by running a line of fabric glue down the center and placing the stems on top of the glue. Chenille stems can also be applied to the edges of the tails or just the tip in the same way. After the glue has dried, bend and curve the tails.

Use fabric glue to add felt spots, stripes, scales, and feathers to the Animal Tunics or color them on with fabric paint or permanent markers.

Collars *(DRAWING 3)*

Use the fanciful collars described in this section on their own or wear them over a tunic costume. Coupled with hats, ears, shoes, or tails, a complete character or animal costume can be created in no time. *(SEE PATTERNS pp. 155–158.)*

Basic Materials

- *felt*
- *paper*
- *hole punch*
- *yarn or ribbon*

Assembly:

1. Cut a rectangular piece of felt or colored construction paper 12"–14" wide but only 16"–18" long.

2. Fold the material in half and use the same procedure for cutting a neck opening.

3. Cut a slit from the center of the opening all the way down the back or front of the material, straight to the bottom *(SEE DRAWING 3)*.

4. For fasteners, punch a hole on either side of the slit and lace yarn or ribbon through the holes to tie closed. For a more decorative

look, punch holes all the way around the neck opening and lace the tie through each hole. Cut the bottom edge of the collars, following the Basic Tunic directions, p. 18 *(SEE DRAWING 3)*.

Add decorations and embellishments to the finished collars, either permanently or temporarily.

SHIRT COLLAR: To make a collar similar to one on a shirt or blouse, cut a collar shape (pointed, rounded, etc.) from felt. Punch a hole in both ends and attach yarn to tie the collar around the neck.

TIE-ON COLLAR: Follow the general directions for making collars to create a collar that ties on, except cut only a front panel. Punch a hole on either side of the neck opening. Thread a piece of yarn through each hole so that the collar can be tied behind the neck. Shape the bottom of the collar and decorate to correspond to the character and costume. Tie-on Collars are especially good for animal costumes, because you can cut and fringe them to resemble fur. Tie-on Collars are not only comfortable and quick to make, they require half the material of other collars.

REVERSIBLE COLLAR: Shirt and Tie-on Collars can be made so that they are reversible. Decorate each side differently so that the collars augment more than one costume or character, depending on which side is worn in front.

Vests *(DRAWINGS 4 AND 5)*

To make a vest, use the Basic Tunic pattern but cut a front opening. *(SEE PATTERNS PP. 159–161.)*

Basic Materials

- *felt*
- *hole punch*
- *yarn, rawhide, or ribbon*

Assembly:

1. Cut a rectangular piece of felt 10"–16" × 24"–26".

2. Fold the piece in half, making a 10"–16" × 12"–13" rectangle. Cut a neck opening as described in step 2 of the Basic Tunic, p. 18.

3. Rather than cutting a short slit in the back, cut a slit from the center of the neck opening all the way down the front.

4. Leave vest open, or fasten by punching several holes on both sides of the front opening. Use yarn, ribbon, or rawhide to lace through both sets of holes for a front closure that can be tied.

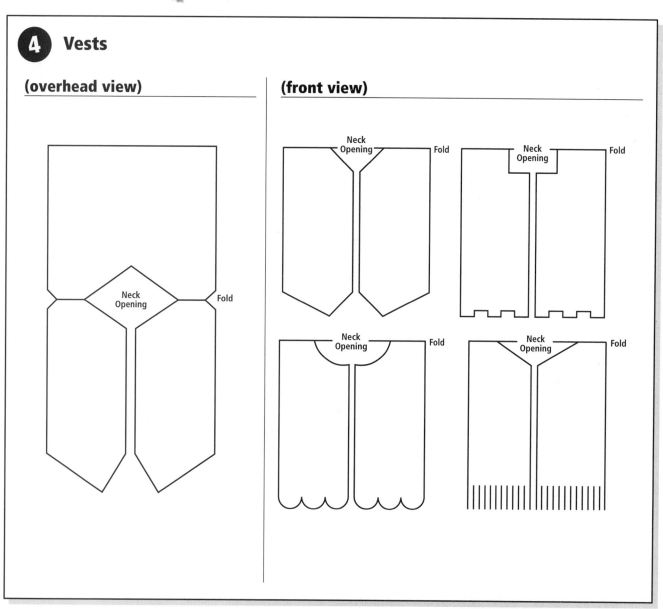

4 Vests

(overhead view)

(front view)

5. Use the techniques described in step 5 of the Basic Tunic to cut the vest bottom.

Add decorations or embellishments as desired. For example, try gluing buttons on one side of the Vest.

BROWN PAPER BAG VEST:

1. Flatten a brown paper grocery bag and use a pencil to mark off an arm hole on each side and a neck opening along the fold.

2. Cut the arm holes and neck opening.

3. Slit the bag up the front, from the bottom to the neck opening. Do nothing to the back of the bag.

4. Remove several inches from the bottom of the bag, to shorten the Vest if necessary. Trim the bottom of the bag with a decorative cut, following the directions for the Basic Tunic. Brown paper bags fringe nicely.

Paper Bag Vests lend themselves extremely well to a variety of decorations and coloring techniques: markers, paint or crayons, sponge painting, stickers, rubber stamps, or glued on pompoms, paper, felt, yarn, ribbon, or foil *(SEE DRAWING 5).*

DIVER VEST: Follow the general directions for making a vest, doubling the length of the front panel. Run two vertical lines (12" long) of fabric glue, two inches apart, on each side of the vest front. Fold the extra length back up to the shoulders, creating a fold on the bottom of the front of the vest. Press firmly on the glued areas. Place a weight on the vest and allow it to dry. This will create four narrow vertical pockets on the vest front. Stuff each pocket lightly with plastic grocery bags, one bag per pocket. Use fabric glue to seal the pockets closed on the top.

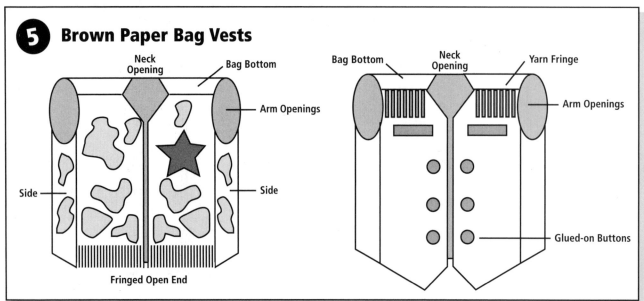

5 **Brown Paper Bag Vests**

Neck Opening — Bag Bottom — Arm Openings — Side — Side — Fringed Open End

Bag Bottom — Neck Opening — Yarn Fringe — Arm Openings — Glued-on Buttons

Capes *(DRAWINGS 6–8)*

A Cape is one of the quickest and easiest costume pieces to make. It is also a favorite of children during pretend play. Again, refer to the instructions for the Basic Tunic, p. 18.

(SEE PATTERNS pp. 162–165.)

Basic Materials

- *felt (or paper bag or crepe paper)*
- *hole punch*
- *yarn or ribbon*

Assembly:

1. Cut an 42"–46" diameter half circle.

2. Fold the semi-circle and cut a neck opening in the center of the straight edge.

3. If desired, punch a hole on either side of the neck opening. Thread a piece of yarn or ribbon through each hole to tie the Cape closed. Or, punch holes all the way around the neck opening and lace the ribbon through each hole before tying. *Note:* On crepe paper and paper bag capes, add adhesive reinforcements to the holes or place a square of tape along the edge before making the holes, to prevent tearing.

4. Cut the bottom edge straight, make a fringe, or use a decorative cut *(SEE DRAWING 6). Note:* It is not necessary to cut a slit, since the half-circle Cape will already have an opening.

Trim Capes (permanently or temporarily) with decorations similar to those used on Basic Tunic costumes.

Idea Starter

SET THE STAGE: Create a stage for Ballerinas (p. 175), Cheerleaders (p. 178), Wizards (p. 190), singing Cowboys (p. 179), or a variety of animal performers. Set aside an area. Use several wooden planks nailed together, a large piece of painted corrugated cardboard, or a small rug as your stage. Make a curtain by draping fabric over a clothesline tied across a corner, position flashlight "spotlights" toward the stage, and add a Microphone (p. 128) and some music.

6 Capes

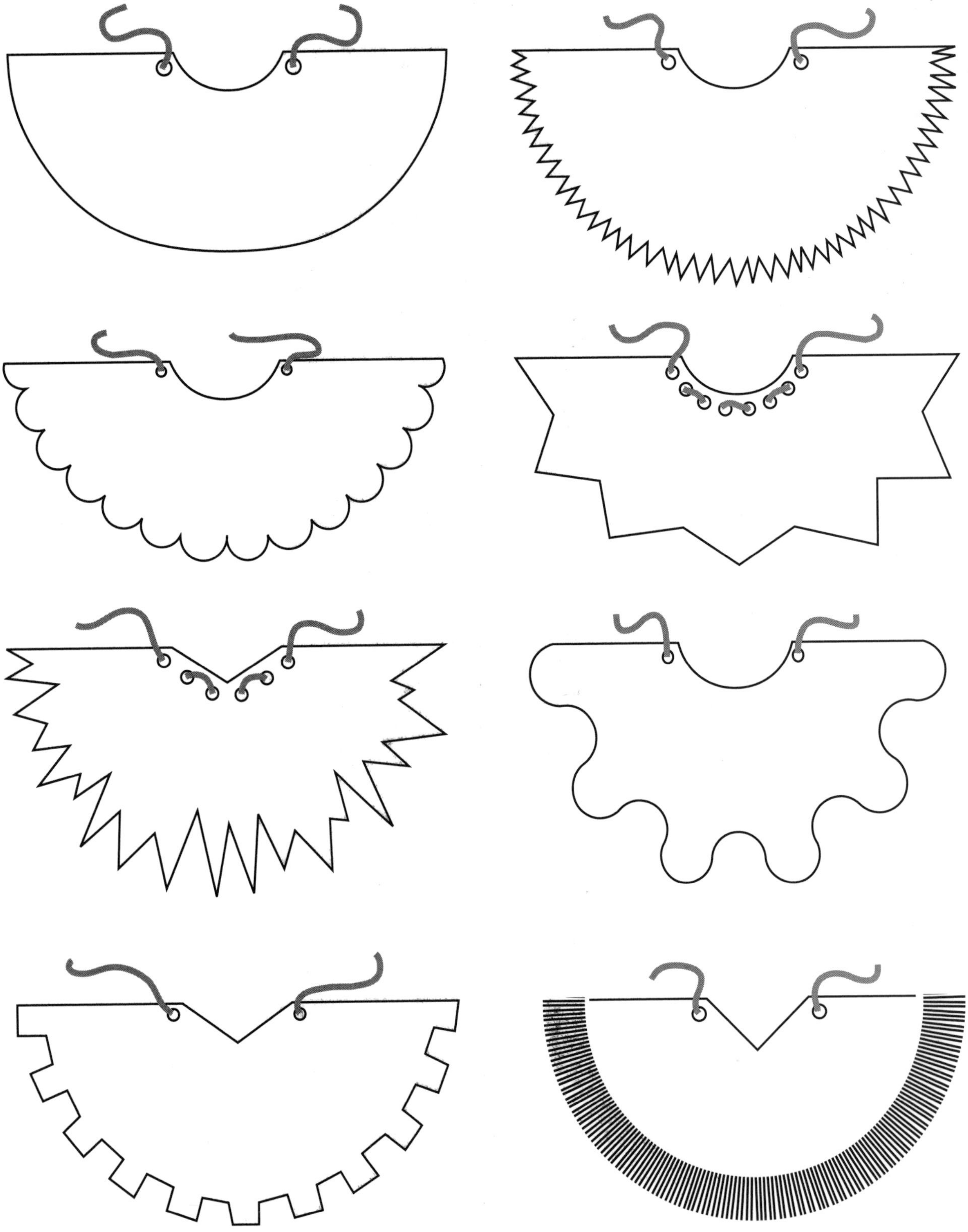

STREAMER CAPE: A fun cape to make and wear is the Streamer Cape.

1. Cut a 30" length of 1"–2" wide ribbon, or cut a strip of felt to this size.

2. Cut twelve to fifteen 36" long strips of crepe paper or ribbon.

3. Attach the 36" strips side by side along the middle 10" of the 30" length of ribbon or felt. To attach the strips, fold each in half, making strips that are 18" long, and place the folded loop under the 30" piece. Bring the ends of each strip up through the loop and pull gently to tighten the strips *(SEE DRAWING 7).* Continue attaching the 36" folded strips in the same way, until all are attached. Use the ends of the 30" length to tie the cape around the neck *(SEE DRAWING 7).*

SCARF CAPE: Use any large-sized scarf for this easy-to-make cape; scarves that are too big or too long can be folded in half first.

1. Lay the scarf flat, and place a piece of yarn across the scarf about 1" down from the top. The yarn should extend 4"–6" on either side of the scarf.

2. Apply a thin line of fabric glue above the yarn, just below the scarf edge *(SEE DRAWING 8).* Fold the glued edge over, creating a casing that allows the yarn to move freely. (The yarn will be between the fold.)

3. Press the glued edge down firmly and set aside to dry.

4. After the glue has dried, gently push the scarf from both ends toward the center while holding the yarn firmly. The scarf will gather along the yarn, to create a Scarf Cape. Use the yarn to tie the cape loosely around the neck *(SEE DRAWING 8).*

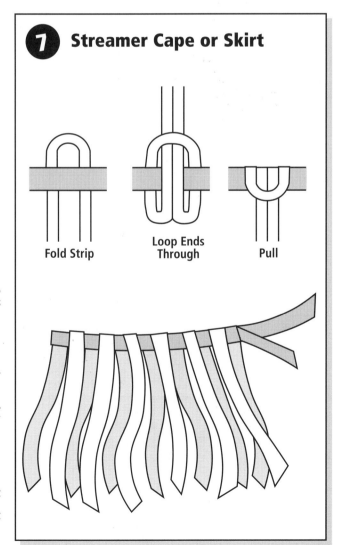

7 **Streamer Cape or Skirt**

Fold Strip

Loop Ends
Through

Pull

Skirts *(DRAWINGS 7–10)*

Skirts are fun costume pieces and should be part of any collection.

STREAMER SKIRTS: Use the procedure for making Streamer Capes to make Streamer Skirts.

1. Cut a 35"–40" length of ribbon, depending on the size needed. A piece of elastic cord works especially well since it stretches to fit any size waist.

2. Cut thirty to thirty-six 40" long (or longer, depending on the desired length of the skirt) ribbon or crepe paper streamers.

3. Attach the looped streamers to the waistband, using more if necessary, as described in steps 3 and 4 for the Streamer Cape, p. 27. Tie the ribbon or knot the elastic to complete the band *(SEE DRAWING 7)*.

SCARF SKIRTS: Follow the basic procedure for Scarf Capes to make Scarf Skirts, except use two to four scarves gathered on one piece of ribbon. Fold the scarves in half for a shorter skirt; leave unfolded for a longer skirt *(SEE DRAWING 8)*.

TULLE (NETTING) SKIRT: Even tulle can be used to make a no-sew costume skirt. Simply refer to the directions for the Streamer Cape and to those that follow.

1. Lay a 35"–40" length of ribbon flat.

2. Cut twenty to thirty strips of tulle, 6" × 24" or 6" × 36" (for a longer skirt).

3. Attach the tulle strips side by side along the ribbon, leaving about 5" on either end for tying. To attach, fold the tulle strips in half, bring ends through the loop and pull gently to tighten *(SEE DRAWING 7)*. Tie the waistband ribbon in the back or on the side, to wear the skirt. Use more tulle strips to make a fuller skirt and use fewer (with more space between each) to make a skirt that is not as full *(SEE DRAWING 9)*.

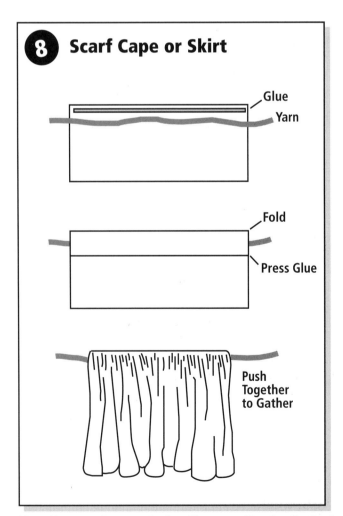

8 **Scarf Cape or Skirt**

Glue
Yarn

Fold

Press Glue

Push Together to Gather

BUBBLE WRAP SKIRT: A skirt of bubble wrap packaging material that has been pleated and attached to a ribbon waistband makes one of the most unusual and fun costume pieces in any collection. Make more than one because this will be a very popular piece!

1. Use bubble wrap from standard packaging, taping small pieces together to create a 12"–16" × 40"–50" sheet. Or, purchase it at a department store, a mailing center, or the local post office. Clear is the most common type, but bubble wrap is also available in lightly tinted colors.

2. Lay the sheet of bubble wrap flat, and fold over 1"–2" pleats across the length of the 40"–50" side. Fasten down each pleat with glue or a piece of clear tape.

3. Lay a 35"–40" piece of ribbon across the taped pleats, positioning it about 1" from the edge and leaving 5"–6" on either end for tying purposes.

4. Secure the ribbon to the bubble wrap with glue or a piece of masking tape or cloth tape. Press firmly to achieve a tight bond. To wear the Bubble Wrap Skirt, simply tie it around the waist, placing the bow in the back or at the side *(SEE DRAWING 10).*

Combine a (Ribbon or Crepe Paper) Streamer Skirt with a Bubble Wrap Skirt by wearing the Streamer Skirt over the Bubble Wrap Skirt, for a different, fancier dress-up piece

9 Tulle (Netting) Skirt

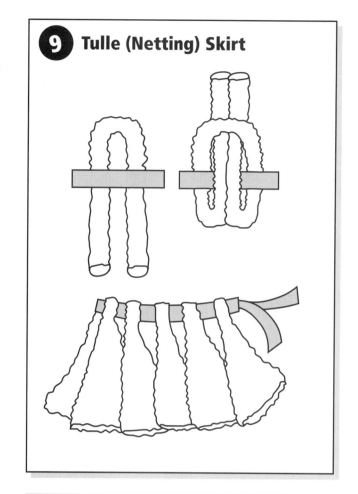

10 Bubble Wrap Skirt

Tape Pleats

Add Ribbon

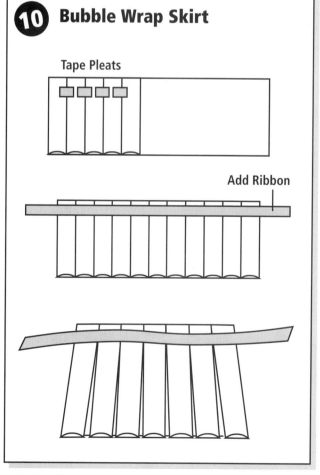

Pillowcase Costumes (DRAWING 11)

By changing the basic structure of a pillowcase just slightly, you can make a number of fun costumes. Use pinking shears to do all of the cutting, to eliminate too much fraying.

Basic Materials
• *pillowcases*
• *markers, fabric crayons, fabric paint, dimensional paint*

Assembly:

1. Holding the pillowcase so that the closed end is at the top, remove both upper corners. Cut at an angle and make the cut about 5"–6" long.

2. Cut a neck opening, also from the closed end.

3. Cut a 6" slit from the center of the neck opening down the middle of the back.

4. Remove several inches from the bottom of the pillowcase to make the costume shorter, as needed.

Pillowcase Costumes are best decorated with permanent markers, fabric crayons, and dimensional paints, or fabric paints. Try any of the following on a Pillowcase Costume (SEE DRAWING 11).

■ animal spots or stripes

■ scales or feathers

■ sports numbers, logos, emblems, or names

■ parts of clothing, such as collars, labels, buttons, and pockets

■ accessories, such as ties, bows, necklaces, badges, and belts

T-shirt Costumes (DRAWING 12)

Oversized T-shirts or adult T-shirts make great costume pieces. The only cutting required is to make length and sleeve adjustments, as needed. Follow the suggestions for Pillowcase Costumes above.

Both Pillowcase Costumes and T-shirt Costumes offer a simple way to expand any dress-up collection. Couple with belts, hats, accessories, and props to create a complete costume that is just as effective as ready-made costumes in stimulating the imaginations of young children. Quick and easy to prepare, enough of these costumes can be made to outfit an entire large group for a dress-up play experience, indoors or out. Also important, they fold flat for easy storage. Check with parents, colleagues, and thrift shops—all are excellent sources of extra pillowcases and T-shirts.

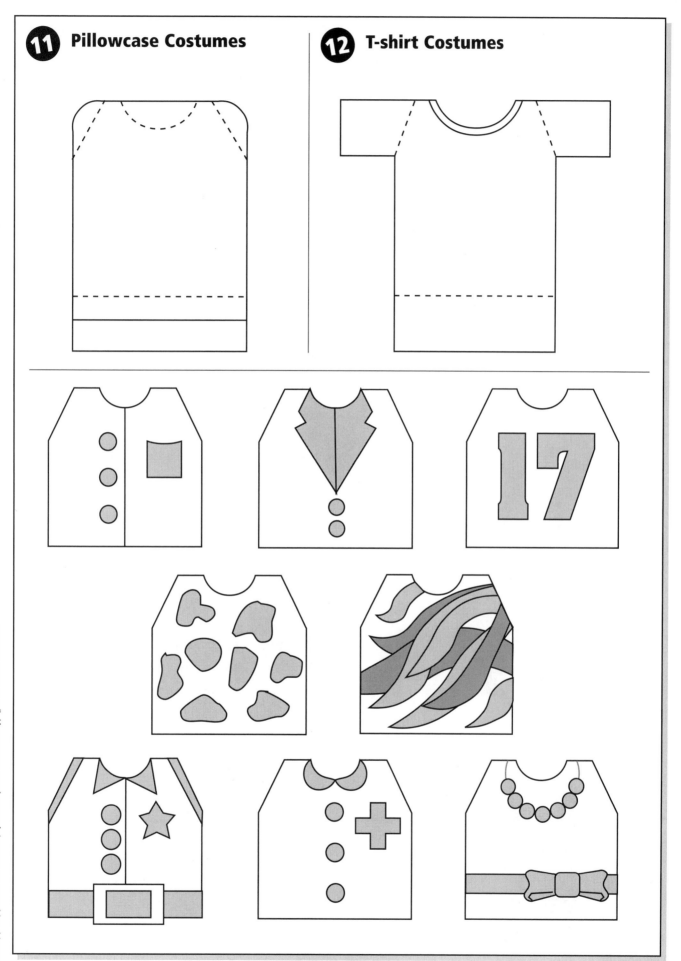

11 Pillowcase Costumes

12 T-shirt Costumes

Don't Forget the Unusual! ....

Enhance costumes and dress-up clothes with unusual items found in the home and at thrift shops or yard sales. Try some of these fun materials:

CARDBOARD TUBES *(from paper towels, aluminum foil, plastic wrap, or gift wrap):* Cut around the tubes diagonally from one end to the other; many tubes have a line to follow when cutting. Spread the resulting spiral apart to fit over forearms and lower legs. Use spray paint or acrylic paint to color the tubes. Dab glue on the tubes and add glitter. Use for space alien, astronaut, and deep sea diver costumes, for example.

CLOTHES DRYER DUCT PIECES: Cut 4" pieces of dryer duct for children to wear on their wrists and ankles. Cut larger pieces to fit on arms and legs. These make an excellent addition to outer-space and underwater pretend play.

METAL COLANDERS AND BOWLS: Turn old metal kitchenware into hats and helmets. Usually, it's just the right size for children's heads. Children really enjoy wearing these items that they usually see elsewhere. Avoid metal pots and pans with handles, for obvious safety reasons.

SHEER CURTAINS AND TABLECLOTHS: Use these items as you would scarves, for capes and skirts. Sheer curtains and small sheer or lace tablecloths also work well as veils and ghost coverings. To make a ghost costume, simply drape the sheer curtain over the head. The sheer fabric is easy to see through and light enough in weight to keep on for extended play.

HOLIDAY TINSEL: Lengths of holiday tinsel can be used in the same way as crepe paper or ribbon to create sparkling capes and skirts. Cut the tinsel into 30"–40" lengths and loop the pieces onto a ribbon or felt strip (see p. 27). Use shorter pieces of tinsel for necklaces and bracelets. Glue lengths of tinsel on tunics, collars, capes, and hats or crowns for added decoration.

CHAPTER

3

Hats, Helmets, and Crowns

Even the most basic costume comes alive when a hat of some kind is added. In this chapter, you'll learn how to make head wear in many shapes and sizes. Some of it is best suited to one particular costume. Much of it, however, can be easily adapted to accompany a variety of costumes. By changing the color of the hat and attaching an assortment of materials, one hat style accommodates a number of different costumes.

As with other costume pieces, make the embellishments permanent with the use of glue—or temporary—with the use of Velcro, tape, or a semi-permanent glue. Look for a variety of suggestions for fastening hats, whether with elastic or yarn ties, brass fasteners, or paper tabs. Note: As in Chapter 2, measurements are presented in a range (such as 16"–18") so that you can choose the size that best suits your needs.

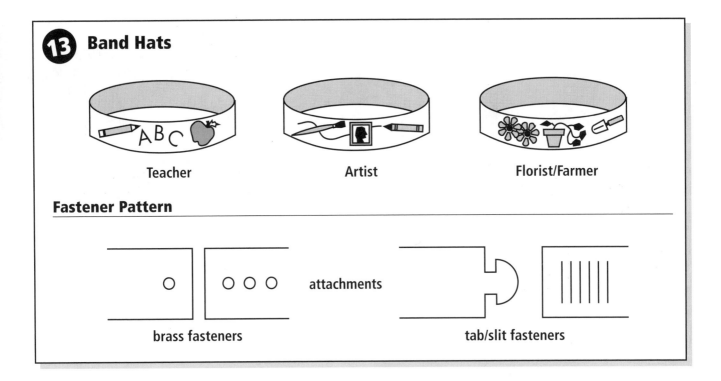

13 **Band Hats**

Teacher   Artist   Florist/Farmer

Fastener Pattern

attachments

brass fasteners   tab/slit fasteners

Band Hats *(DRAWING 13)*

This hat serves a variety of purposes and can be made in minutes. Attach symbols that suggest characters or occupations to the band. Children will enjoy being involved in the planning and construction of Band Hats, both brainstorming symbols associated with occupations and making the hats. Band Hats are a wonderful way to add something distinctive to characters that have less identifiable uniforms or accessory pieces.

Assembly:

1. Cut a 3" × 20"–24" forehead band.

2. Punch one hole in one end and several holes in the other so that the band can be adjusted to fit children's heads. Attach with brass fasteners. Or, fasten by cutting a tab in one end and a series of slits, $\frac{1}{2}$" apart, in the other end. Use a utility knife to cut the slits. Insert the tab into the slit that best secures the Band Hat on the child's head.

Florist

From *Nifty, Thrifty, No-Sew Costumes & Props* published by Good Year Books. Copyright © 1998 Good Year Books.

Decorate:

■ Add an embellishment to make the hat look like a real hat. For example, glue on a foil circle to make the hat look like a doctor's examination hat.

■ On each band, tape or glue three to five symbols that represent a character or occupation. Draw the symbols yourself or cut pictures from magazines and catalogs.

Variations:

Try these picture suggestions to make Band Hats for the following occupations.

■ **ARTIST:** various art tools, framed art, smocks, paint

■ **BARBER:** scissors, comb, brush, mirror, various heads of hair

■ **CAR MECHANIC:** cars, trucks, tires, gas pump, oil cans

■ **CARPENTER:** various tools, ruler, tape measure, paintbrush, house

■ **CASHIER:** coins, money, cash register, sales tags, paper bags

■ **DENTIST:** teeth, mouth, toothbrush, toothpaste

■ **FARMER:** various plants and farm animals, garden tools, plow, tractor, barn, scarecrow

■ **FLORIST:** various plants and flowers, trees, watering can, seed packets, bouquets, spade

■ **LIBRARIAN:** various books, library cards, ink pad, ink stamp, pencil

■ **MUSICIAN:** various musical instruments, music stands, written music, microphone

■ **SECRETARY:** typewriter, computer, telephone, paper, pens, file folder

■ **TEACHER:** pencil, ABCs, ruler, chalk, books, school building, apple

■ **VETERINARIAN:** various pets and animals, eyedropper, thermometer, pet bowls, pet food

■ **WEATHER FORECASTER:** various kinds of weather, umbrella, maps, sunglasses, snow shovel, boots

■ **ZOOKEEPER:** various animals (wild and tame), cages, broom, pail, zoo sign

Felt Band Hats *(DRAWING 14)*

Like a Band Hat, a Felt Band Hat is worn around the forehead. Use a variety of colors, coordinating them to match colors of tunics, collars, and vests. The embellishment or decoration that makes each Felt Band Hat distinctive is placed on the front of the band. Glue it on permanently, or use Velcro, tape, or a semi-permanent glue to attach the decoration temporarily. Paper clips also work well for temporarily attaching the distinguishing features.

(SEE PATTERN P. 166.)

Basic Materials

- *felt*
- *poster board or lightweight cardboard*
- *hole punch*
- *yarn*
- *clothespins for clamping*

Assembly:

1. Cut a 3" × 20"–24" band from poster board. Curve the center of the band to a 5"–6" height. This will hold the hat decoration.

2. Cut an identical band from felt.

3. Glue the felt band on top of the poster board band. Use spring clothespins to clamp the band firmly while it dries.

4. Punch a hole in either end of the band and tie a piece of yarn in each hole. Use the yarn to secure the Felt Hat Bands on the head. Or, use Velcro or elastic cord to attach. If using Velcro, place one piece of self-stick Velcro on one end and several pieces on the other end so that adjustments can be made. If using elastic, shorten the length of the band to 14"–16" and punch a hole in both ends of the band. Secure the elastic between the holes so that the Felt Band Hat can be slipped over the head.

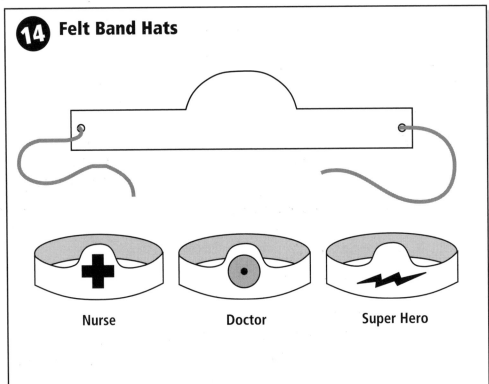

14 Felt Band Hats

Nurse   Doctor   Super Hero

Decorate:

- Cut a variety of attachments from felt, poster board, or construction paper. Magazine or catalog pictures can also work well so long as they are mounted on heavier paper first. Relate the embellishment to the character or occupation being portrayed: a Red Cross, a star, a flag, a 911 badge, or other emblem.

- Combine other materials with the felt or poster board shapes, such as foil, glitter, plastic gems, sequins, pompoms, or flowers (SEE DRAWING 14).

- Decorate with facial features to make an animal headpiece.

Point Hats (DRAWING 15)

The Point Hat can be worn in a number of different ways on the head. It is made with only one strip of cardboard and can be left plain or decorated.

Basic Materials

- *poster board or light-weight cardboard*
- *stapler*

Assembly:

1. Cut a 4" × 20"–24" strip of poster board.

2. Trim both ends to a curve or point.

3. Bend the strip and attach the ends with a stapler. Do not overlap the ends. The point can be positioned over the forehead, to the side, or in the back.

Decorate:

- Color the poster board strip with markers before assembly.

- Glue tissue paper scraps onto the strip before assembly.

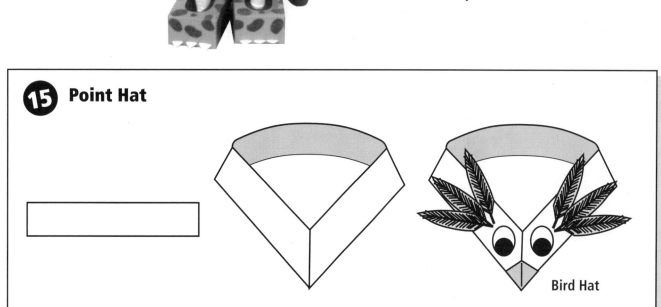

15 **Point Hat**

Bird Hat

- Attach emblems, badges, stars, and other items to Point Hats to suggest various occupations such as hot dog or ice cream vendor and military officer. Paper clips can be used to secure items, so that hats can be reused many times.

Variation:

- **BIRD HAT:** Make a Point Hat to go along with a bird costume. Position the point in the front, add an eye on either side of the point, color the point yellow or orange, and decorate the sides and back of the hat with feathers *(SEE DRAWING 15).*

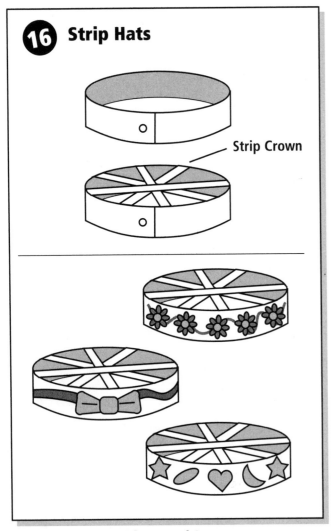

Strip Hats *(DRAWING 16)*

Make this hat out of construction paper strips, using one color or an assortment of colors. Attach a variety of decorations, badges, or emblems to make hats distinctive.

Basic Materials

- *construction paper*
- *hole punch*
- *brass fasteners*
- *tape, glue, or stapler*

Assembly:

1. Cut a 2" × 20"–24" forehead band.

2. Make one hole in one end and several holes in the other end of the band so that the band can be adjusted to fit the child's head. Attach with brass fasteners. Or, fasten by cutting a tab in one end and a series of slits, $\frac{1}{2}$" apart, in the other end. Use a utility knife to cut the slits. Insert the tab into the slit that best secures the Strip Hat on the child's head.

3. Cut four to six 2" × 10" strips.

4. Tape, glue, or staple both ends of each strip to the inside of the forehead band. Crisscross the strips across the top of the hat to form the crown area.

Decorate:

- Glue tissue paper flowers, felt flowers, or artificial flowers around the band and on the strips.

- Glue felt, paper, or tissue paper shapes on the band and strips.

- Add bows or glitter to Strip Hats.

Variations:

From *Nifty, Thrifty, No-Sew Costumes & Props* published by Good Year Books. Copyright © 1998 Good Year Books.

- Cover white paper strips with colorful gift wrap before assembly.

- Use wallpaper strips instead of construction paper.

- Attach holiday trims, such as tinsel on paper strips and forehead bands to make a fancy Paper Strip Crown (SEE DRAWING 16).

Visor Hats (DRAWING 17)

Visor Hats are easy to make and can be used with many different costumes and types of dress-up clothes. Make multiples of the Visor Hat in a variety of colors and materials. (SEE PATTERN P. 167.)

Basic Materials

- *poster board or light-weight cardboard*
- *hole punch*
- *brass fasteners*
- *glue*

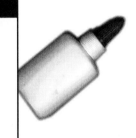

Assembly:

1. Cut a 2" × 20"–24" forehead band.

2. Trace the visor pattern onto poster board and cut it out. Fold the straight side and make several cuts into it, but not through it.

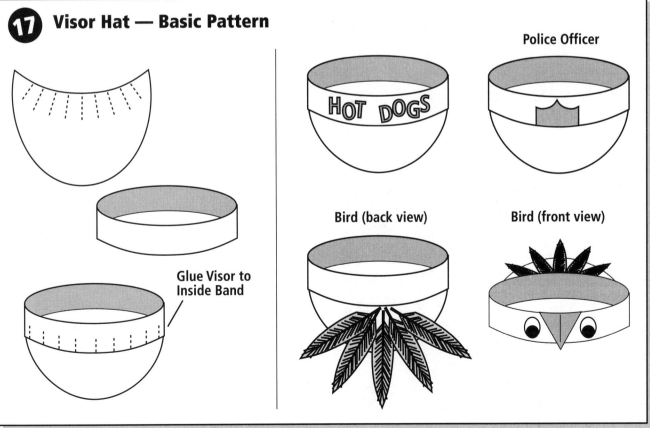

17 Visor Hat — Basic Pattern

Glue Visor to Inside Band

Police Officer

HOT DOGS

Bird (back view)

Bird (front view)

3. Apply glue to the cut end and attach the visor to the middle of the forehead band.

4. Punch one hole in one end and several holes in the other end of the band so that it can be adjusted to fit children's heads. Attach with brass fasteners, or by cutting a tab in one end and placing a series of slits, $\frac{1}{2}$″ apart, in the other end. Use a utility knife to cut the slits. Insert the tab into the slit that best secures the Visor Hat on the child's head.

Decorate:

■ Use markers, crayons, or paints to color visors.

■ Cut gift wrap, wallpaper, or colored construction paper to fit the visor front. Attach the paper with glue.

■ Decorate new and old visors with a variety of items such as flowers, emblems, pompoms, or felt shapes.

Idea Starter

WEAR A HAT—DO A JOB: Give any child a special hat to wear while doing a chore and the "work" immediately takes a playful turn! In a classroom or other group setting, each day's chosen helpers can wear a special hat. For example, children who help with cooking or passing materials to the group can wear a Restaurant Worker (p. 189) hat or a Mail Carrier (p. 186) hat. In the home, a child can wear a Restaurant Worker hat to help set the table or dry the dishes, a Police Officer (p. 188) hat to bring bikes and riding toys inside, or a Sombrero (p. 44) or Sun Hat (p. 44) to help water plants or work in the garden.

Variations:

■ **BIRD HAT:** Cover the visor front with feathers. Attach with glue. Glue eyes and a beak on the front of the forehead band. Children wear the hat with the visor in the back.

■ **FIRE HAT:** Cut a 12″ diameter oval from black poster board. Trace a 6″ diameter circle in the center and then cut only three-fourths of the way around the circle. Fold the attached section up and trim it to the desired size. Cover the folded up portion with red felt. Add a yellow felt badge to the red felt. Attach both with glue.

■ **PIRATE HAT:** Use the pattern, p. 168, to cut two pirate hat shapes from poster board. Then cut four felt pieces, using the pattern. The felt pieces can be all black or two each of black and gray. Glue the felt pieces onto the poster board, covering the front and the back. Cut an X shape from white felt and glue it to the front of the hat. Place the pieces on top of each other and staple, several inches in from both ends.

Cone Hats *(DRAWING 18)*

Numerous costumes make use of a Cone Hat—such as a wizard, a princess, an elf, or a clown. The variety of decorations that can be added to a Cone Hat make it suitable for birthday dress-ups or animal and character costumes.

Basic Materials

- *construction paper*
- *tape*
- *hole punch*
- *yarn, elastic cord, or ribbon*

Assembly:

1. Cut a 10"–12" diameter circle from construction paper.

2. Cut into the circle halfway.

3. Roll the circle into a cone shape and secure with tape. Trim the uneven edges and cut off any excess paper from the inside of the cone.

4. Punch a hole in each side of the Cone Hat. Place yarn or ribbon through each hole so that the hat can be tied under the chin. A piece of elastic cord secured through the holes works well as a chin strap.

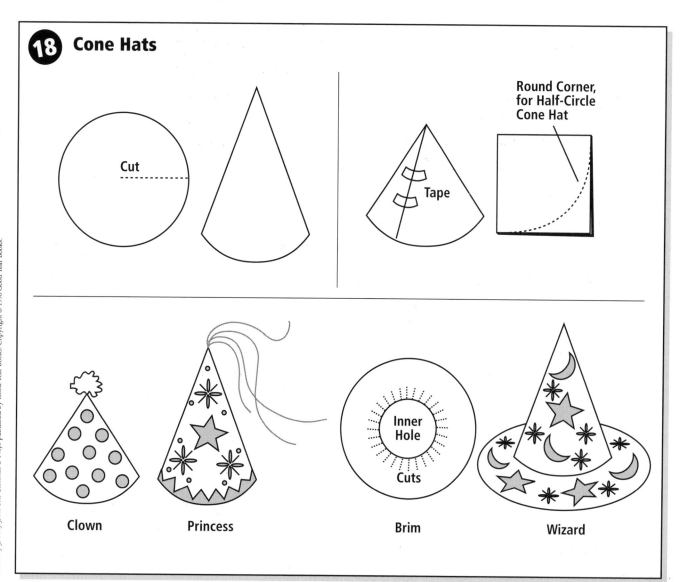

18 Cone Hats

Cut

Tape

Round Corner, for Half-Circle Cone Hat

Clown

Princess

Inner Hole

Cuts

Brim

Wizard

Decorate:

- Use markers or crayons to decorate.

- Glue gift wrap or wallpaper to the construction paper circle before beginning. Roll into a cone and attach with tape.

- Glue stickers, glitter, pompoms, or tissue paper flowers to the Cone Hat.

- Fasten a pompom or a tassel to the pointed top (perfect for a Clown Cone Hat).

Variations:

- **HALF-CIRCLE CONE HAT:** A Cone Hat can also be made with a 12" × 18" piece of construction paper. Fold the paper in half so that it measures 9" × 12". Round one of the corners with scissors so that the paper, when opened, forms a half circle. Roll the half circle into a cone and fasten it with tape or staples.

- **PAPER PLATE CONE HAT:** Follow the basic procedure for a Cone Hat, except use a large paper plate. Makes a smaller-sized Cone Hat.

- **PRINCESS CONE HAT:** Attach several pieces of ribbon or crepe paper to the point of a tall Cone Hat. Decorate the hat with glitter, foil shapes, or stars.

- **WIZARD CONE HAT:** Follow the directions for the Cone Hat using an 18" circle of (black or purple) construction paper. To make a brim, cut a second circle, 10"–12" in diameter, and remove a 6"–8" diameter circle from the center. Clip a 1" fringe around the center circle. Bend the fringe up and tape the brim to the inside edge of the Wizard Cone Hat. Put foil stars and crescents and dots of glitter all over the hat.

Brims and Brimmed Hats
(DRAWING 19)

Brims and Brimmed Hats can accommodate a variety of looks and can be worn with many costumes. By varying the size of the brim and changing the style of the top, you can create a number of different hats such as a Top Hat, Western Hat, or Floppy Hat. The Brim Hat can also be worn without a top to create a Sombrero or Beach Hat, a Sun Hat or Boat Hat, or a Three-Cornered Hat.

Basic Materials

- *poster board or light-weight cardboard*
- *tape*
- *hole punch*
- *yarn, ribbon, or elastic cord*

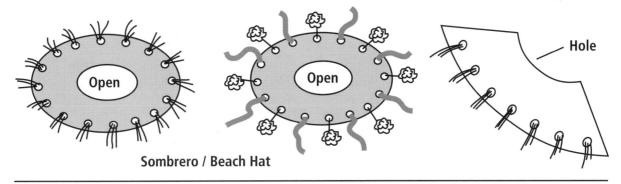

Sombrero / Beach Hat

Hole

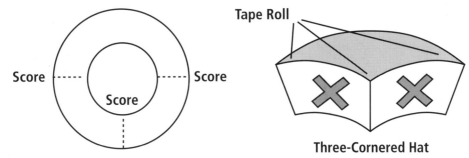

Score — — — Score

Score

Score

Tape Roll

Three-Cornered Hat

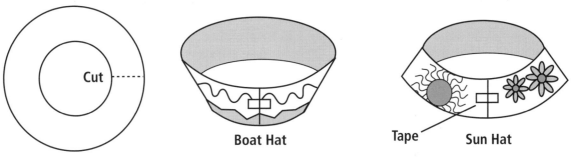

Cut — — —

Boat Hat

Tape

Sun Hat

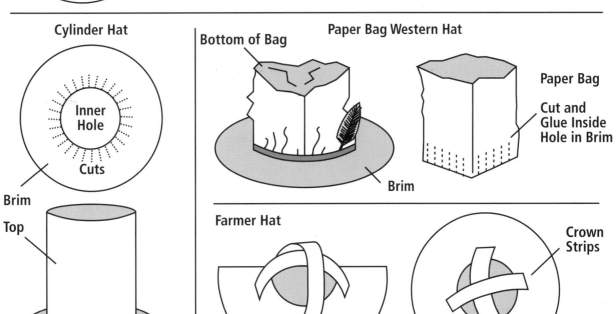

Cylinder Hat

Inner Hole

Cuts

Brim

Top

Paper Bag Western Hat

Bottom of Bag

Brim

Paper Bag

Cut and Glue Inside Hole in Brim

Farmer Hat

Crown Strips

Assembly:

1. Cut a 12"–16" diameter circle from poster board and remove a 6"–8" diameter hole from the center. For a broader Brim, cut a larger circle; for a narrower Brim, cut a smaller circle. The 6"–8" center hole remains the same size.

2. Punch a hole on both sides of the Brim near the inner circle. Attach yarn or ribbon through each hole so that the Brim can be tied under the chin. Or, secure with elastic cord instead.

3. Use Brim as is or connect Brim to different style hat tops. To attach Brims to hat tops, clip a 1" fringe around the inner circle of the Brim and bend the clipped edge up. Attach the clipped edge of the Brim to the inside edge of the hat top with glue or tape.

Decorate:

- Coordinate the colors of the Brims with those of the hat tops.

- Cover both sides of the Brim with felt for a sturdy, realistic hat.

- For a more colorful hat, cover the Brims with wallpaper or gift wrap.

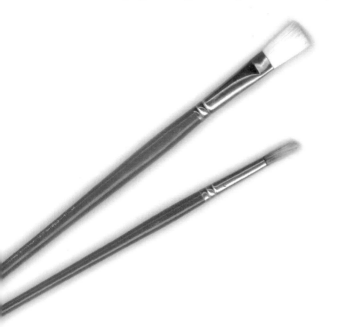

Variations:

- **SOMBRERO OR BEACH HAT:** Make a brim only, leaving the crown area open. Punch holes at 2" intervals around the edge of the brim. Decorate the edge in any of the following ways: tie two 3" pieces of yarn in each hole to create a fringe; lace ribbon or crepe paper in and out of the holes for a fancy trim; tie a pompom in each hole; add bells or paper flowers.

- **BOAT HAT OR SUN HAT:** Construct a brim from a 15" diameter circle, removing a 6"–8" diameter inner circle. Cut straight through one section of the brim. Overlap the cut edges and tape or staple. Wear with the brim turned up for a Boat Hat and with the brim facing down for a Sun Hat. Decorate with acrylic or dimensional paint, or with markers. Or, try covering the hats with gift wrap, wallpaper, or felt cut to the same size.

- **THREE-CORNERED HAT:** Make a brim from a 15" diameter cardboard circle, removing a 6"–8" diameter center circle. Score the brim three times, making two 5" sections and one 10" section. To score cardboard, use a utility knife and lightly cut into, but not through, the cardboard. (Scoring makes the cardboard easier to bend.) Bend all three scored lines out to form the hat (SEE DRAWING 19). Place rolled tape between the upper corners of the three scored sides to hold the shape of the hat. Decorate with foil disks or felt shapes. Or, try covering the Three-Cornered Hat with felt, cutting three individual pieces and gluing one to each side.

- **CYLINDER (TOP) HAT:** Begin with a cardboard brim made from a 12"–14" diameter circle with a 6"–8" diameter inner circle removed. Out of construction paper, cut a 12"–18" wide and 8"–12" long rectangle, depending on the desired height of the Cylinder Hat. Tape the 12"–18" edges of the rectangle together. Clip a 1" fringe around the center circle of the brim. Bend the clipped edge up and attach it to the cylinder with glue or tape. Make a top for the hat by clipping the top end of the cylinder, bending it, and taping it to a circle cut the same size as the opening. Hat bands and feathers look great on Cylinder (Top) Hats *(SEE DRAWING 19).*

- **PAPER BAG WESTERN HAT:** Begin with a 12"–14" diameter cardboard circle brim with a 6"–8" diameter inner circle removed; use brown cardboard or cover cardboard with brown paper from a grocery bag or brown construction paper. For the top, cut a brown paper grocery bag in half horizontally, making a shorter bag. Clip a 1" fringe along the open end of the bag and bend the fringe back. Fit the clipped edge of the bag into the center circle of the brim. The opening of the bag will be larger than the circle. You will need to gather and pleat the bag as you attach it to the brim with glue or tape. Crease and form the bag into the shape of a Western Hat. Decorate the Paper Bag Western Hat with a hat band, rope, red bandanna, or feather *(SEE DRAWING 19).*

- **FARMER HAT:** Cut a 12"–14" diameter cardboard circle brim, removing a 6"–8" diameter inner circle. Cut four 2" × 10" strips of construction paper. Fasten them across the inner circle by taping 1"–2" of each strip on the underside of the inner circle, creating a crisscross crown area. Punch a hole on both sides of the hat near the center and tie a ribbon or piece of yarn in each hole so that the Farmer Hat can be tied under the chin. Decorate Farmer Hats with flowers, ribbons, hay, or wheat. *(SEE DRAWING 19).*

Bonnets *(DRAWING 20)*

Make a very sturdy pull-on hat that needs no ties under the chin. By varying the paper and trims, a number of different looks can be achieved.

Basic Materials

- *wallpaper or heavy-duty gift wrap*
- *glue and water mixture (2 parts glue to 1 part water)*
- *large rubber band*
- *medium-sized bowl*

Assembly:

1. Cut two 16"–18" squares of wallpaper or heavy-duty gift wrap.

2. Spread the glue and water mixture generously over the back of one of the squares. Place the other square face up on the glue, securing so that the squares are glued back to back and the design is visible on both sides.

3. Spread more of the glue/water mixture on top of the glued square. The wallpaper or gift wrap should be fairly wet.

4. Turn the bowl upside-down. Mold the square over the bowl, positioning the wet side to the outside. Use fingers to smooth the paper over the bowl.

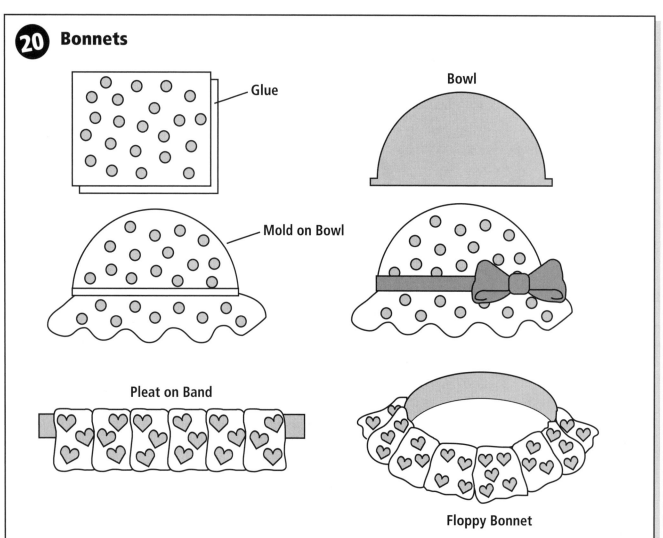

20 Bonnets

Glue

Bowl

Mold on Bowl

Pleat on Band

Floppy Bonnet

5. Place a large rubber band around the rim of the bowl. Pleat the wet paper to fit as needed. The rubber band will hold the paper in place and give the Bonnet some shape as it dries. Be sure the brim of the hat hangs below the bowl.

6. Let the paper dry on the bowl. Remove the rubber band. Trim the brim.

Decorate:

- Wrap a ribbon around the brim and tie it in a bow at the side, or attach a bow only.

- Add a large flower on the side or small flowers all the way around the Bonnet.

Variations:

- **FLOPPY BONNET:** Use a forehead band as the base for this hat, cutting a 3" × 20"–24" strip of construction paper. Then cut a 5" × 48" strip of wallpaper, gift wrap, crepe paper, or felt. Making 2" pleats, staple the strip onto the forehead band. Be sure to place the smooth side of the staples next to the skin and to line up the edges of the pleated strip with the edge of the forehead band.

- **LACE BONNET:** Cut five to seven 6" diameter paper doilies in half. (You will need fewer if doilies are larger.) Pleat and staple the doilies to a forehead band, following the directions for the Floppy Bonnet. Decorate the Lace Bonnet with flowers, feathers, pompoms, and ribbon.

Make tops for Floppy Bonnets and Lace Bonnets with four 2" × 10" strips of construction paper. Tape 1" of each end of the strips to the underside of the forehead band, forming a crisscross pattern that will fit over the crown of the head.

Idea Starter

CROWNS FOR BIRTHDAYS: Plan a birthday party around a costume theme. The birthday child can wear a Crown (p. 51) or a Tiara (p. 53) and become the King, Queen, Prince, or Princess of the party. Make Cone Hats (p. 41) or smaller Crowns for party guests to wear. Give each guest a party favor: a Medallion (p. 108), a Collar Necklace (p. 107), or a Felt Pouch (p. 123) filled with foil-covered chocolate coins, candies, and a small toy.

Papier-Mâché Hats *(DRAWING 21)*

This hat takes a little more time to make, but the result is a sturdy, long-lasting costume piece that complements any dress-up collection. Involve children in the construction process. They particularly like dipping the newspaper strips and applying them to the inflated balloon.

Basic Materials

- *newspaper*
- *glue and water mixture (2 parts glue to 1 part water)*
- *large round or oval balloon*
- *straight pin*

Assembly:

1. Tear newspaper into 10"–12" strips.

2. Dip the strips in the glue/water mixture and slide them through the fingers to remove excess liquid. Place the strips on an inflated and securely tied balloon. Overlap the strips, covering the balloon completely.

3. Apply four to six layers, allowing drying time between each layer.

4. Dry overnight.

5. Place a pin in the area where the balloon is tied. When the balloon has deflated, remove it.

6. Use scissors to cut the papier-mâché form into a bowl-shaped hat. If the balloon is large enough, it may be possible to cut two hats from one form.

7. Paint and decorate the Papier-Mâché Hat.

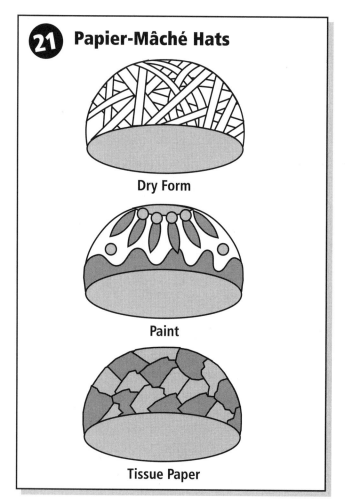

㉑ Papier-Mâché Hats

Dry Form

Paint

Tissue Paper

Decorate:

- Paint Papier-Mâché Hats with an acrylic paint. A base coat of white paint first will yield a more even, vivid final color. Try brushing on a sealer (on dry paint) for added durability.

- Apply a three-dimensional or puffy paint on top of the painted hat, if desired. Make lines, dots, shapes, flowers, or other pictures.

- Use glue to attach feathers, felt shapes, tissue paper flowers, tassels or beads, and sequins on top of painted hats.

Variations:

- Instead of a balloon, use a bowl, pot, or cookie tin to form the Papier-Mâché Hats. Cover the outside of the container with a thin coat of petroleum jelly or cooking oil and cover the greased surface with plastic wrap before applying the newspaper strips. Dip newspaper strips in the glue/water mixture and place them on the prepared container. Overlap the strips and apply four to six layers, allowing drying time between layers. When the last layer is dry, remove the papier-mâché form, trim the edge, paint, and decorate.

- Use torn fabric strips instead of newspaper to cover the balloon. The procedure is the same, except that drying time may be a bit longer. The finished hat needs no painting. Decorate with flowers, feathers, or ribbons.

- Use tissue paper strips in place of newspaper strips, for a thinner, more fragile hat. Apply six to eight layers, allowing drying time between each layer. The finished hat needs no painting. Decorate with tissue paper flowers, ribbons, or feathers (*SEE DRAWING 21*).

From *Nifty, Thrifty, No-Sew Costumes & Props* published by Good Year Books. Copyright © 1998 Good Year Books.

Twist Hats *(DRAWING 22)*

This clever hat is made without stitching, tape, or glue of any kind. The Twist Hat is soft and somewhat stretchy, giving it a snug and comfortable fit.

Basic Materials

- *tights or opaque pantyhose (a great use for something that might otherwise be thrown away)*
- *yarn*
- *material for stuffing: cotton, shredded paper, or fiberfill*

Assembly:

1. Cut both legs from the tights.

2. Remove the feet and cut two 16"–20" lengths from the legs.

3. Tie a knot in both legs, 2" from the end of each.

4. Stuff both legs until they are full and firm.

5. After stuffing, tie a knot 2" from the other end, making two separate coils.

6. Lay the coils side by side. Tie two ends together with yarn.

7. Twist the tied coils together like a braid. Use yarn to tie the two free ends together.

8. Form a circle with the braided coils and tie all four ends together with yarn. Knot securely. Wear the Twist Hat around the forehead and back of the head.

Decorate:

- Weave a string of plastic beads or ribbon loosely through the braided coils.

- Glue felt flowers or artificial flowers to the Twist Hat.

- Tuck feathers into the braided coils.

Variation:

- **SINGLE COIL HAT:** Make a single coil only, tying the ends together with yarn to form a circle. Wear plain, decorate with beads, feathers, or flowers. Wrap a print scarf or ribbons diagonally around the coil and tie in a bow or a knot to secure *(SEE DRAWING 22)*.

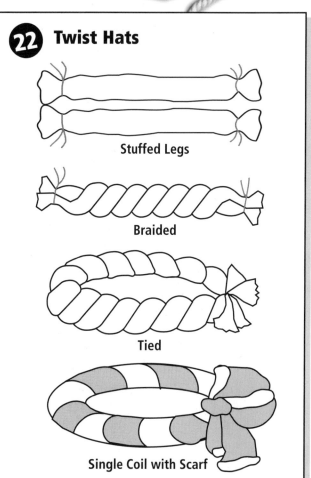

22 **Twist Hats**

Stuffed Legs

Braided

Tied

Single Coil with Scarf

Helmets (DRAWING 23)

These are as fun to make as they are for children to wear. Use lots of imagination and whatever materials you have on hand to decorate the Helmets. Depending on the decorations selected, Helmets can be made to accompany costumes depicting a number of diverse characters, such as astronauts, firefighters, and deep-sea divers.

Basic Materials

- *plastic milk or water jugs, thoroughly washed and rinsed (one-gallon size)*
- *masking tape*

Assembly:

1. Cut the top from a one-gallon plastic jug.

2. Cut an oblong section from the open end of the jug down toward the bottom of the jug, removing the handle. The opening should be about 4"–5" wide and 5"–6" high, so that the child's whole face will show through it when he or she turns the jug upside down and places it on the head. Cut a 1" strip from the back of the jug to provide a looser fit.

3. For safety and comfort, sand the cut edges lightly to make them smooth, or cover the edges with masking tape; use colored tape on the edges for an added decorative touch.

Decorate:

- Use colored tape to add stripes to the Helmets.

- Attach chenille stems for antennas.

- Glue on pompoms and shapes cut from felt or aluminum foil.

- Use brass fasteners to attach paper and cardboard "knobs" that will really turn.

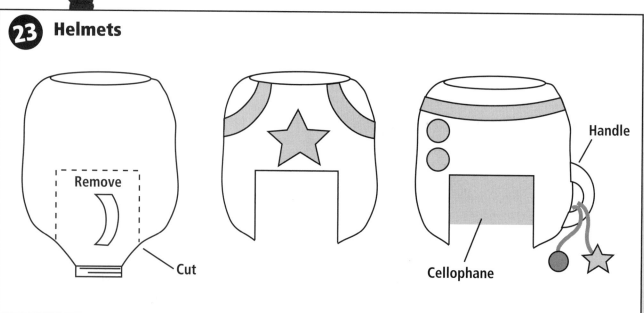

23 Helmets

Remove

Cut

Handle

Cellophane

From *Nifty, Thrifty, No-Sew Costumes & Props* published by Good Year Books. Copyright © 1998 Good Year Books.

- Use acrylic paint or try a puffy, dimensional paint to add stars, numbers, and letters to Helmets. Apply a sealer on top of the paint.

Variations:

- Tape a narrow strip of colored cellophane or plastic wrap from one side of the opening to the other so that it covers the eye area when the Helmet is worn. This is particularly appropriate for an astronaut or outer space costume.

- Rather than remove the handle section of the jug, preserve it and cut the oblong face opening so that the handle is positioned at the side of the head. The handle becomes an added feature. Try painting it, hanging objects from it, or gluing cardboard "knobs" or "buttons" on it.

- **KNIGHT HELMET FACE GUARD:** Use black poster board to cut a 10"–12" long diamond shape that will fit across the cut opening in the helmet. Fold the diamond in half and cut four to six slits in the fold. Place a hole in each end of the diamond and in both sides of the plastic jug. Attach the diamond face guard to the helmet with brass fasteners.

- **CONSTRUCTION HARD HAT:** Remove the entire top of a one-gallon, plastic water or juice jug. Cut straight around the jug from the base of the handle. Paint the remaining bottom of the jug with orange acrylic paint. Apply a sealer to keep paint from chipping.

- Construct Helmets out of large ice-cream containers (cardboard or plastic). Remove any metal or plastic rim and cut a face opening in the front, as previously described. Try covering with aluminum foil before decorating *(SEE DRAWING 23).*

Crowns and Tiaras *(DRAWING 24)*

No dress-up area is complete without Crowns, and they need not all be fancy. Whether it is the traditional cut-and-fasten crown or a more involved construction, this is a very popular dress-up accessory.

(SEE PATTERNS P. 169.)

Basic Materials
• *poster board or light-weight cardboard*   • *hole punch*   • *brass fasteners*

Assembly:

1. Choose one of the crown patterns provided or create one of your own. Trace the pattern onto 20"–24" long poster board. Position the Crown so that the design is in the center and allow a 2" wide strip on either side of the design.

2. Cut out the Crown.

3. Punch one hole in one end and several holes in the other so the Crown can be adjusted to fit children's heads. Attach with brass fasteners, or by cutting a tab in one end and a series of slits, $\frac{1}{2}$" apart, in the other end. Use a utility knife to cut the slits. Insert the tab into the slit that best secures the Crown on the child's head.

Decorate:

■ Use markers, crayons, or paint to decorate. Draw circles, ovals, diamonds, triangles, stars, or crescents on the front.

■ Draw lines, dots, and shapes, such as those listed above, in glue. Sprinkle on glitter. Allow to dry and shake off the excess.

■ Cut aluminum foil or other foil paper into any small shapes and glue shapes to the front.

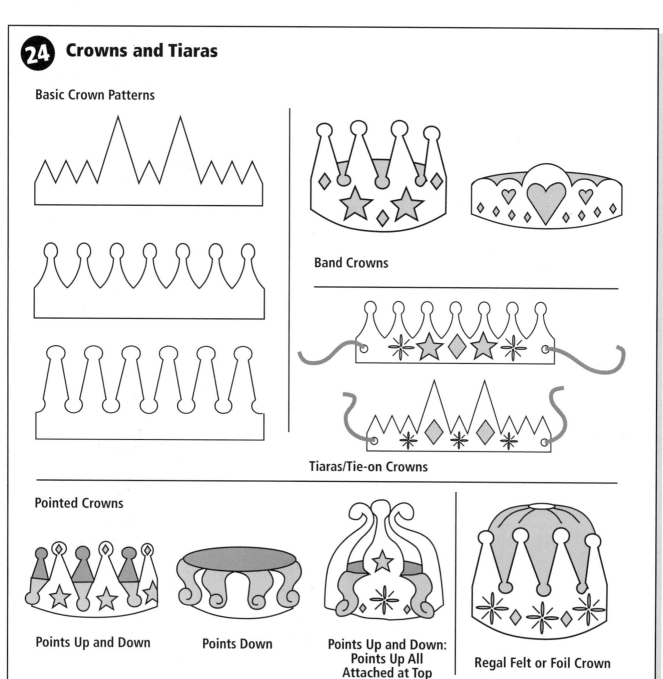

24 Crowns and Tiaras

Basic Crown Patterns

Band Crowns

Tiaras/Tie-on Crowns

Pointed Crowns

Points Up and Down | **Points Down** | **Points Up and Down: Points Up All Attached at Top** | **Regal Felt or Foil Crown**

From *Nifty, Thrifty, No-Sew Costumes & Props* published by Good Year Books. Copyright © 1998 Good Year Books.

- Cover the front of the Crown with a piece of foil before cutting it out. Glue glitter and/or sequins on top of the foil.

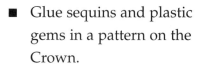

- Glue sequins and plastic gems in a pattern on the Crown.

- Shape 3" pieces of various colors of chenille stems to form stars, diamonds, crescents, and hearts. Attach the stem forms to the Crowns with glue.

- Gently pull and flatten cotton balls. Attach them with glue around the band of the Crown, for a white fur look. Glue plastic gems, sequins, and glitter on the points of the Crown.

Variations:

- **TIARA/TIE-ON CROWN:** Make Tiaras or Tie-on Crowns by tracing only the crown front onto cardboard, eliminating the ends that would wrap around the head. Punch a hole on both sides of the Tiara. Place yarn or ribbon through each hole and tie the Tiara at the back of the head or use elastic and tie one end through each hole. Cover with felt or aluminum foil and decorate by glueing on jewels.

- **POINTED CROWN:** Construct a Crown with points all the way around. Use the pattern provided on p. 169, or create a different one. Use either means just described for fastening Pointed Crowns on the head.

    Leave points on the Crown straight. Or, curl points with the blade of scissors. Curl points so that they face forward, and glue the tip of each point to the base of the Crown. Try alternately gluing or taping points onto the base of the Crown. Gather together those points not glued down, and secure over the Crown (SEE DRAWING 24).

- **REGAL FELT CROWN:** Make one of the band crowns and then add a puffy interior covering made from a circle of felt. Cut a 12"–14" diameter circle of felt. Attach the felt circle to the inside of the band with glue and tape as follows: Pleat the felt circle so that it fits the band; apply glue to each pleat; press a piece of cloth tape or masking tape over the pleats, attaching them to the band for added stability. Match the colors of felt used on the crowns to capes, collars, and tunics. When children wear the Regal Felt Crown, the felt stands above the top of the head.

- **REGAL FOIL CROWN:** Instead of felt, use heavy-duty aluminum foil. Cut a 12"–14" diameter circle of foil and attach it, shiny side out, to the band of the Crown. Pleat or fold the foil as needed to fit the band. Press the folds flat, gluing them to the inside of the band. Place a piece of tape over the glued foil to keep it secure.

    For a very Regal Crown, combine jeweled or glittered points with a felt or foil head covering and a cotton "fur" band (SEE DRAWING 24).

CHAPTER 4

Eyes, Noses, Ears, Wigs, and Beards

Costume pieces for the face offer opportunities for more involved role play and further development of characters, animals, and fantastic creatures. Children will enjoy using these accessory pieces to change their identity and alter their appearance. Remember, mirrors are an important part of any dress-up area, allowing children to witness their transformation as they don a new costume. When accessories for the face are added to the area, mirrors are a MUST.

Make several sets of the facial accessories described in this section, changing colors and decorations as needed to ensure an adequate supply and varied choices. Another good way to alter appearances (without the use of masks) is by using make-up or face paint. The Money-Saving Recipes chapter (Chapter 9) presents several home-made, nontoxic recipes for this purpose—see, for example, Fantastic Face Paint and Skin Glue and Skin Designs.

Eyes

Eye Bands (DRAWING 25)

Basic Materials

- *poster board or light-weight cardboard*
- *construction paper*
- *glue*
- *hole punch*
- *brass fasteners*

Assembly:

1. Cut a 2" × 20"–24" forehead band with two "eye coverings" extending down from the center of the band. Eye coverings can come in a variety of basic shapes—circles, diamonds, and so on, and should be large enough to cover the eyes and extend to the cheekbone.

2. Cut an eye hole in the center of each eye covering.

3. Punch several holes in each end of the forehead band so that it can be adjusted to fit children's heads. Attach with brass fasteners. Or, fasten by cutting a tab in one end and a series of slits, $\frac{1}{2}$" apart, in the other end. Use a utility knife to cut the slits. Insert the tab into the slit that best secures the Eye Band to the child's head.

25 Eye Bands

Cut Holes

Variations:

- Cover Eye Bands with any color paper that best suits the creature being portrayed. Glue on cut paper shapes to outline the eyes, and add eyelashes, spots, stripes, scales, and feathers.

- Add a nose, trunk, or beak to Eye Bands by cutting the feature directly into the bottom of the band, between the two eyes, or by connecting it to the bottom of the eyes.

- Cut thin paper strips or stiffen small yarn pieces with liquid starch. Glue them on either side of the nose to make whiskers.

- Add ears, paper hair, a bow, or even a hat to the Eye Band in much the same way. In this case, cut the items directly into the top of the band, above the eyes.

- Combine a number of the features described, such as whiskers, a nose, hair, or a bow and ears, on one Eye Band for a complete head covering.

Egg Carton Eyes *(DRAWING 26)*

Basic Materials

- *egg carton (cardboard works best)*
- *yarn or elastic cord*
- *hole punch*

Assembly:

1. Cut two sections from an egg carton, leaving them intact as one piece.

2. Cut an eye hole in the bottom of each section.

3. Punch a hole in both sides of the egg carton section. Knot a piece of yarn through each hole so that the Egg Carton Eyes can be tied behind the head. Or, tie one end of a piece of elastic cord in each hole so that the eyes can be slipped over the head.

Variations:

- Tape a piece of colored cellophane over the eye hole in the bottom of each section.

- Cut two 1"–2" paper fringes. Glue the fringes on the top of each egg cup section as eyelashes.

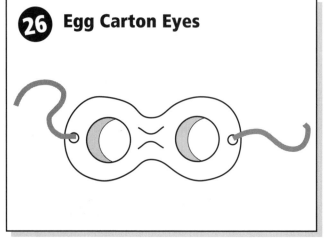

26 **Egg Carton Eyes**

Plastic Ring Eyes *(DRAWING 27)*

Basic Materials

- *plastic six-pack rings*
- *yarn*

Assembly:

1. Cut two adjoining rings from a six-pack holder.

2. Tie yarn on both sides of the rings. Use the yarn to fasten the Plastic Ring Eyes by tying them behind the head.

Variations:

- Tape a circle of colored cellophane on the back of each adjoining ring to make colored eyes.

- Cut two 1"–2" paper fringes and glue one to the top of each ring to make eyelashes.

- Trace the two adjoining rings onto construction paper and cut out. Glue the paper rings on top of the plastic rings. Add cellophane or leave plain.

- Make Animal Eyes by adding stripes, spots, or fur (color in or cut out and attach) to paper rings before cutting them out and gluing them to the plastic rings.

- **TIGER:** glue black felt stripes on orange felt rings or color black stripes with markers

- **ZEBRA:** glue black stripes on white paper rings or use markers

- **LEOPARD:** glue black circles on yellow paper rings or use markers

- **SNAKE:** glue brown, black, and red scales on green or yellow paper rings or use markers

- **BEAR:** cut out brown paper rings with a zigzag edge to suggest fur

- **PANDA BEAR:** cut out a smaller ring of black and glue it to a larger ring of white or use markers

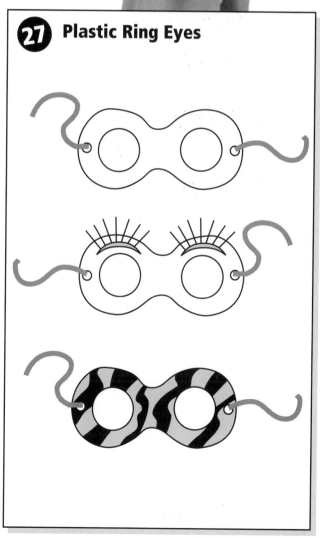

27 Plastic Ring Eyes

Paper Cone Noses *(DRAWING 28)*

Basic Materials

- *construction paper*
- *tape*
- *yarn or elastic cord*
- *hole punch*

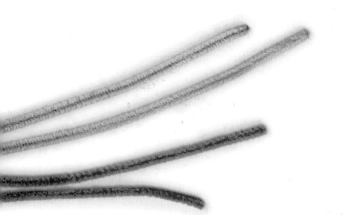

Idea Starter

COSTUME SONGS: Combine a variety of animal costumes with well-known songs for a role-play music experience. When you sing a song such as "Old MacDonald," "Farmer in the Dell," or "Over in the Meadow" with children, give them the opportunity to wear animal costumes that relate to the song characters. As you sing about each animal in the song, the costumed child can do motions and make animal sounds. Children can wear a full costume or one costume piece (ears, a tail, paws) —particularly effective with large groups, since more children can have turns. Substitute animal names in songs to match your costume collection.

Assembly:

1. Cut a 2" or 3" diameter circle.

2. Cut into the circle halfway.

3. Roll the circle into a cone. Tape the edge and trim the bottom. Trim off any excess paper inside the cone.

4. Punch a hole on both sides of the cone. Attach a piece of yarn through each hole and use the yarn to tie the Cone Nose around the head. Or, tie each end of a piece of elastic cord in the holes so that the nose can be slipped over the child's head.

Variations:

- **MATCH THE COLOR OF PAPER TO THE ANIMAL:** use gray for a mouse, brown for a squirrel, and yellow or orange for a bird.

- **MAKE WHISKERS FOR THE NOSE:** Use the tip of a pair of scissors to make three or four holes on both sides of the Cone Nose. Cut six to eight 3" pieces of yarn. Knot one end of the yarn and dip the knotted end in glue. Place the unknotted end through the hole from the inside of the cone. Pull the yarn until the knotted (and glued) end catches in the hole. The glue will help keep these "whiskers" snug. Or, make whiskers out of 3" pieces of chenille stem. Attach the stems with glue in the same way as the yarn pieces, except bend the ends that are inside the cone.

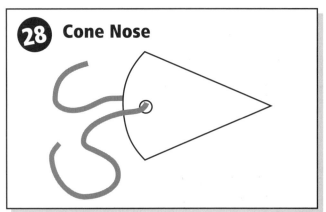

28 **Cone Nose**

Egg Carton Noses *(DRAWING 29)*

Basic Materials

- *egg carton*
- *adhesive bandages*

Assembly:

1. Cut one egg cup from an egg carton.

2. Cut off the sticky end of an adhesive bandage and roll it up, sticky side out. Use the rolled piece of bandage to attach the Egg Carton Nose. (Adhesive bandages stick well and are gentle to skin.)

Variations:

- Use markers or paint to embellish the egg cup.

- Glue cotton or felt shapes (circles, ovals, triangles) on the end of the Egg Carton Nose to make noses for rabbits, cats, dogs, bears, and other animals.

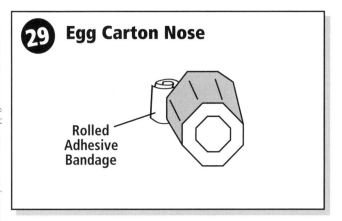

29 Egg Carton Nose

Rolled Adhesive Bandage

Paper Cup Noses *(DRAWING 30)*

Basic Materials

- *small paper cup*
- *hole punch*
- *yarn or elastic cord*

Assembly:

1. Cut a small paper cup in half (horizontally), making a shorter cup.

2. Punch a hole in both sides of the cup. Attach a piece of yarn through each hole and use it to tie the Paper Cup Nose behind the head. Or, tie each end of a piece of elastic cord in the holes so that the Paper Cup Nose can be slipped over the child's head.

Variations:

- **ANIMAL NOSES:** Cut a strip of construction paper to fit around the outside of the cup and a circle to fit the bottom. Glue the paper to the cup before punching the side holes and adding the yarn. Match the color of paper to the animal being portrayed—for example, pink for a pig nose and brown or white for a bear nose.

- **CLOWN NOSE:** Cut a strip of red paper to fit around the outside of the cup. Crumple a second piece of red paper to form a ball. Spread glue on the bottom of the paper cup and place the paper ball on the glue.

30 **Paper Cup Nose**

Ears

Headband Paper Ears (DRAWING 31)

Basic Materials

- *plastic headband*
- *construction paper*
- *glue or tape*

Assembly:

1. Fold construction paper in half and cut out two animal ears. The ears should be 2"–3" wide and 3"–4" high, or larger for longer ears. Position the bottom of the ears on the fold so that the end result is a double ear joined by a fold in the center (SEE DRAWING 31).

2. Wrap each paper ear around the top of a plastic headband.

3. To secure, use two rolled pieces of tape between the wrapped ears: one at the base next to the headband and one at the end, or tip, of the ear. Taped ears can easily be removed from the headband, and new ones attached. To make paper ears more permanent, spread glue on the inner surface of one side of the ear, from the tip of the ear to the headband. Press the front and back of the ear together to attach.

Variations:

- Cut the edges of the paper ears with pinking shears or use regular scissors and cut in irregular points, to suggest fur. Or, fringe the edges to achieve a furry appearance.

- Edge paper ears with chenille stems the same color as the ears, to suggest fur and to make the ears sturdier.

- Use markers and paper stripes or spots attached with glue, to make ears more realistic.

- Glue light pink or white paper inner ears on the fronts of the paper ears before attaching them to the headband.

- Glue a small piece of cotton on the fronts of the ears to suggest inner ears.

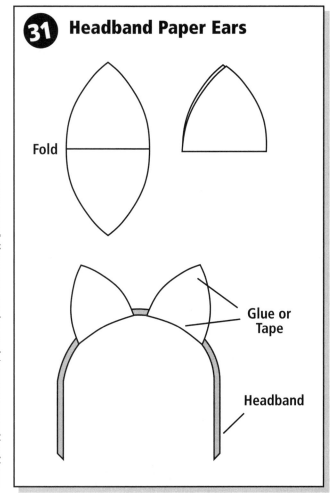

Headband Felt Ears (DRAWING 32)

MATERIALS

- *plastic headband*
- *felt square (9" × 12")*
- *fabric glue*
- *chenille stems*

Assembly:

1. Fold felt in half and cut out two animal ears measuring 2"–5" in width and 3"–4" in height, or larger for longer ears. Position the bottom of the ears on the fold so that the end result is a double ear joined at the fold.

2. Wrap each felt ear around the top of a plastic headband.

3. Cut two pieces of chenille stem, each 2" long.

4. To secure stems to ears, spread fabric glue along the stems and place one stem vertically in the center of each ear, between the fold. (When the ears are dry, the chenille stems enable shaping and positioning of the ears.)

5. To secure ears, apply fabric glue to the ears, about $\frac{1}{4}$" from the edge, and to the headband, where the ears meet it. Press the fronts and the backs of the ears together firmly. Use spring clothespins to hold in place until the glue dries.

6. Shape and position ears as appropriate.

   Note: To make felt ears that can be removed from the headband and exchanged with a different set of ears, glue or staple only the top edges of the ears. Omit the chenille stems between the ears. Instead, stuff cotton into the base of the ears, next to the headband. This adds form to the ears while keeping them from drooping forward or sliding off the headband.

Variations:

- Cut the edges of the felt with pinking shears or use regular scissors to cut the edges in points to suggest fur. Or, fringe the edges of the felt to achieve a furry appearance.

- Glue felt stripes and spots of a different color on the felt ears before attaching the ears to the headband.

- Glue pink or white felt inner ears on the fronts of the felt ears before attaching them to the headband.

- Glue a small section of cotton on the fronts of the ears to suggest inner ears.

- **HORSE MANE:** Attach a mane on the headband between the horse ears. Cut two strips of felt 3" × 18" and one strip 3" × 12". Cut a wide fringe in both ends of the three strips, placing the cuts 3" up one end and 7" up the other end on the short strip, and 3" and 13" up either end on the long strips. Leave 2" uncut. Glue the 2" uncut sections, one on top of the other, on the headband between the ears. Place the 3″ fringe in the front, and the long fringe down the back as a mane.

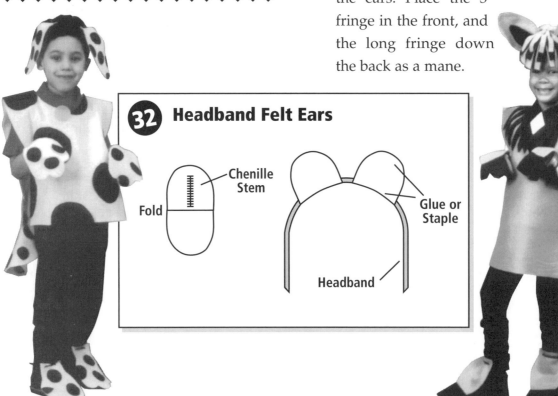

32 Headband Felt Ears

Chenille Stem

Fold

Glue or Staple

Headband

From *Nifty, Thrifty, No-Sew Costumes & Props* published by Good Year Books. Copyright © 1998 Good Year Books.

Papier-Mâché Ears *(DRAWING 33)*

Basic Materials

- *plastic headband*
- *newspaper*
- *glue and water mixture (2 parts glue to 1 part water)*

Assembly:

1. Tear newspaper into strips (any size).

2. Dip the strips into the glue/water mixture and pull them through the fingers to remove any excess liquid. Wrap the strips around the headband once, allowing the extra length of the strips to hang off the top of the band. Wrap two sections of strips where the ears will be positioned.

3. Wrap four to six layers total, allowing drying time between each layer. The layered areas should be about 2" wide. No need to be concerned with the length or shape of the ears, since the ears will be trimmed when the layers are dry. While the layers are still damp, use fingers to shape them and add dimension.

4. After the last layer has dried, trim layered sections with scissors to the final ear shape. Cut with regular or pinking shears.

5. Paint and decorate the finished ears.

Decorate:

- For best results, paint the Papier-Mâché Ears with acrylic paints (tempera paint may also be used). A base coat of white paint first will yield a more even, vivid final color. Try brushing on a sealer (on dry paint) for added durability.

- Apply a dimensional, puffy paint on top of white or painted ears to make stripes, spots, fur, and other details.

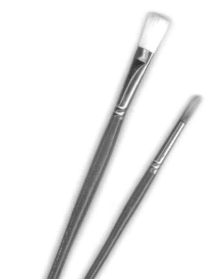

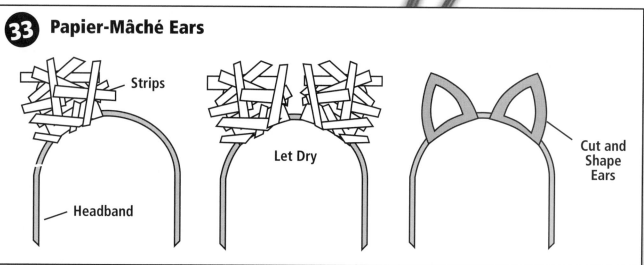

33 **Papier-Mâché Ears**

Strips

Let Dry

Cut and Shape Ears

Headband

From *Nifty, Thrifty, No-Sew Costumes & Props* published by Good Year Books. Copyright © 1998 Good Year Books.

Variation:

■ Instead of wrapping strips directly over a headband, make Papier-Mâché Ears that are detachable and interchangeable by applying newspaper strips to a balloon. Follow the directions for making a Papier-Mâché Hat (p. 47). When the last layer of newspaper has dried and the balloon has been deflated, cut the ear shapes directly from the balloon shape. Try to match the curve of the balloon to the curve of the ears. Depending on the size of the balloon, you may be able to cut two or three pairs of ears from one papier-mâché form. Paint and decorate the ears. Attach them to the plastic headband with a piece of tape on both the front and the back of the ears.

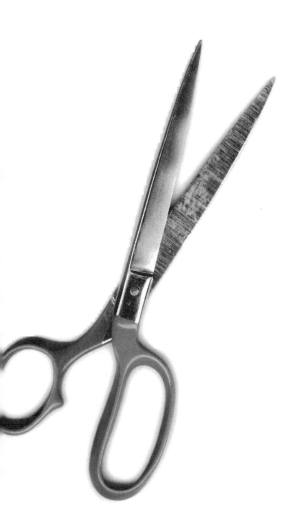

Wigs

Wig Bands *(DRAWING 34)*

Basic Materials

- *poster board or light-weight cardboard*
- *hole punch*
- *brass fasteners*
- *glue*
- *yarn*

Assembly:

1. Cut a 2" × 20"–24" strip of poster board.

2. Punch several holes in both ends of the strip so that the band can be adjusted to fit children's heads. Attach with brass fasteners.

3. Cut forty to sixty yarn pieces, twenty to thirty for each side of the band. Or, for enough yarn to go all the way around the band, double this number. Depending on the thickness of the yarn and the spacing on the forehead band, more or less yarn can be used. The length of the hair needed for the wig will determine the length of the yarn pieces that will be cut: 3"–4" for shorter hair, 5"–8" for medium-length hair, and 9"–12" for long hair.

4. Cut fifteen to twenty-five 1"–2" pieces of yarn for the front of the hair, or the bangs. This is the part of the wig that will hang above the eyes.

5. Spread glue generously on the portion of the forehead band that will be covered with hair, either on the middle 10"–12" or all the way around the band.

From *Nifty, Thrifty, No-Sew Costumes & Props* published by Good Year Books. Copyright © 1998 Good Year Books.

6. Lay the yarn pieces side by side on top of the glue-covered band, keeping one end of the yarn even with the top edge of the forehead band. Glue the shorter pieces of yarn in the center and the longer pieces on either side. Press on the yarn to secure and let the band dry completely before wearing. You may want to weight down the Wig Band during drying time.

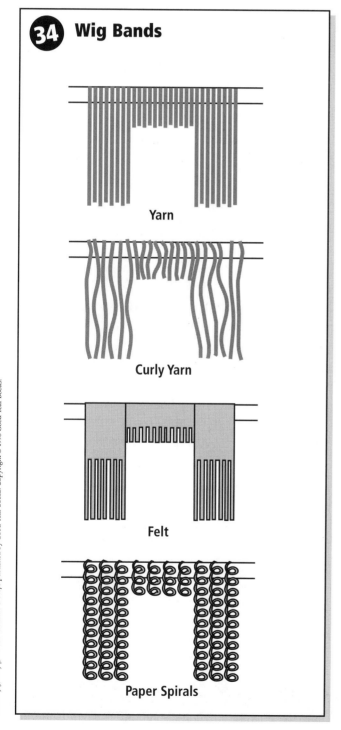

34 **Wig Bands**

Yarn

Curly Yarn

Felt

Paper Spirals

Variations:

- Try using other materials for hair on Wig Bands: string, ribbon, crepe paper strips, straw, or raffia.

- **CURLY WIG BAND:** Dip the yarn in liquid starch and wrap it around a pencil, dowel rod, or paper towel tube (depending on the curl size desired) to dry. Cut longer lengths of yarn, since curling will shorten the hair somewhat. When the yarn is dry, remove the pencil, rod, or tube and glue the hair to the band following the preceding directions.

- **BRAIDED WIG BAND:** Braid several strands of yarn on each side

- **FELT WIG BAND:** Cut strips of felt, about $\frac{1}{4}$" wide, and glue to the forehead band one strip at a time. Or, fringe two 4" pieces of felt. Glue to each side of the forehead band. The length of the felt strips will depend on the desired hair style.

- **PAPER WIG BAND:** Cut $\frac{1}{2}$"–1" strips of construction paper and glue to the forehead band one strip at a time. Or, fringe two 4"–6" pieces of paper and glue to each side of the forehead band. Leave paper hair straight or curl it by wrapping it around a pencil, cardboard tube, or other round object.

- **PAPER SPIRAL WIG BAND:** Cut 3"–4" diameter paper circles: cut into each circle about $\frac{1}{4}$", then cut around to the center of the circle without cutting off any of the circle. Cut sixteen to twenty spirals for each side of the band. Glue the center of the cut circles to the forehead band, letting the spirals hang down like curls. For bangs, attach a 2" paper fringe to the center of the band. Or, cut individual smaller spirals for this section.

Headband Hair *(DRAWING 35)*

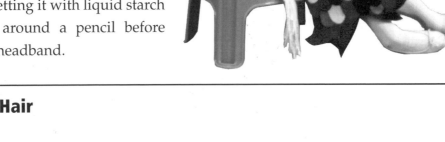

MATERIALS

- *headband*
- *yarn*
- *liquid starch*

Assembly:

1. Cut thirty to fifty pieces of yarn, 24"–36" in length.

2. Knot the yarn on the headband by folding each piece in half, laying the folded loop under the headband, and then bringing the ends up over the headband and through the loop. Pull on the ends to tighten the yarn on the headband. To make a fuller wig, add more yarn pieces.

3. Trim the ends. Keep the yarn hair straight or curl the yarn by wetting it with liquid starch and wrapping it around a pencil before attaching it to the headband.

Variation:

- **BRAIDS:** Tie three strands of yarn, 24"–36" in length, to each side of a headband. Fold the strands in half and loop all three at once onto the headband, following the instructions for Headband Hair. After looping you will have six 12"–18" pieces of yarn to braid. Repeat for the other side. Knot the loop on the outside of the headband. Separate the six pieces into three groups of two each and braid the yarn from top to bottom. Use more loops of yarn for a thicker braid. Fasten the braids at the ends with ribbon, yarn, or a rubber band.

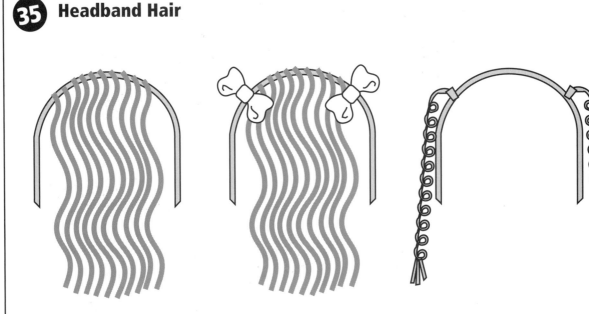

35 Headband Hair

Mustaches *(DRAWING 36)*

Make mustaches out of a variety of materials. Attach them to the face with rolled adhesive bandages. Cut the pad from the center of the bandage and roll up the two ends, sticky side out. Fasten one roll to each side of the mustache or fasten one roll to the center of the mustache, then place the mustache on the face. Try any of the following materials to make fun costume mustaches:

- **CHENILLE STEMS:** Cut two 3" pieces of chenille stem. Twist together in the center and curve the ends up or down.

- **RAFFIA:** Cut a 2" bundle of raffia. Tie the bunch together in the center with a small piece of raffia or yarn.

- **FAKE FUR:** Cut small scraps of fake fur or fleece into 2"–3" strips, shaping the ends into upward or downward curves.

- **COTTON:** Stretch out a cotton ball on both ends. Twist the center and shape the two ends as desired.

- **YARN:** Soak six 2"–4" pieces of yarn in liquid starch. Pull the yarn through the fingers to remove the excess liquid. Separate the yarn into two groups of three pieces each and tie together in the center. Lay the tied yarn on a piece of waxed paper to dry.

- **FELT:** Cut a mustache shape from felt. Clip tiny fringes along the bottom.

- **POSTER BOARD:** Cut a mustache shape from poster board or lightweight cardboard. Fringe the bottom or keep it straight. Color the mustache with markers or crayons.

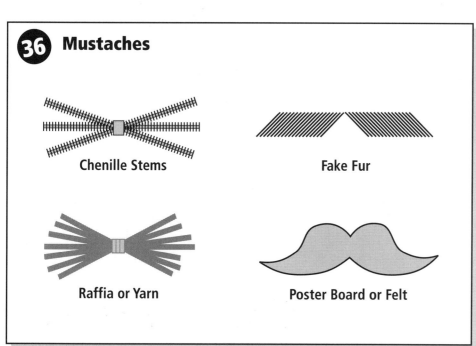

36 Mustaches

Chenille Stems

Fake Fur

Raffia or Yarn

Poster Board or Felt

Poster Board Beards

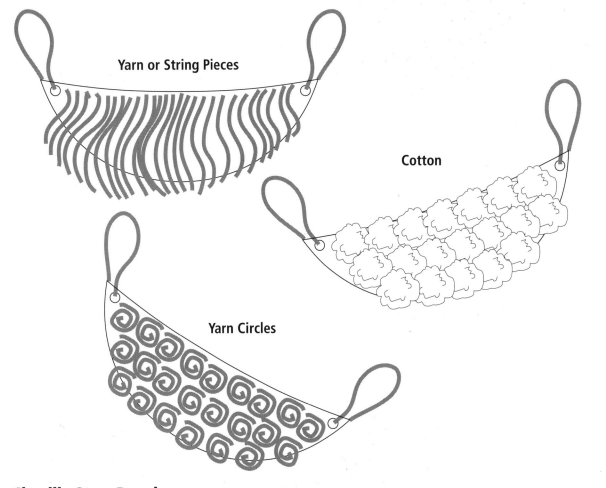

Yarn or String Pieces

Cotton

Yarn Circles

Chenille Stem Beards

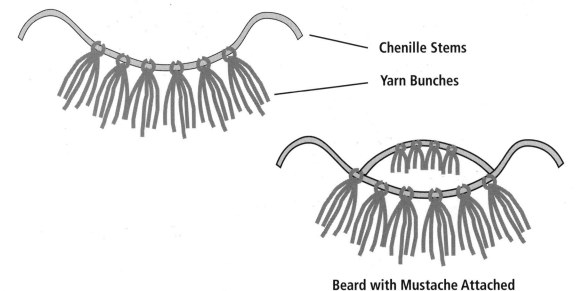

Chenille Stems

Yarn Bunches

Beard with Mustache Attached

From *Nifty, Thrifty, No-Sew Costumes & Props* published by Good Year Books. Copyright © 1998 Good Year Books.

Beards *(DRAWING 37)*

Make beards out of a variety of materials for a quick, easy disguise. Attach yarn loops to the beards by punching a hole in each side of the crescent and tying a 4"–6" loop of yarn through each hole. Children wear the beards by hanging the yarn loops over the ears.

Poster Board Beards

Cut a 6" diameter circle from poster board or lightweight cardboard. Cut the circle in half. Remove a portion of each half circle, to make a crescent shape. (One circle makes two crescents, and thus two beards.) Spread glue on the crescent and cover it with any of the following:

- cotton
- straight yarn or string pieces
- yarn or string circles
- strips of felt
- raffia
- fake fur or fleece
- paper strips
- paper curls

Chenille Stem Beards

Cut yarn into 12"–16" pieces. Make twenty to thirty bundles, eight pieces of yarn to each bundle. Use a small piece of yarn to tie each bundle onto one long chenille stem. Tie the bundles side by side until the stem is covered. Twist a chenille stem onto each end of the yarn-covered stem. Shape the ends of the attached stems so that they fit around the ears (like the stems of eyeglasses). Adjust the end stems around the ears so that the beard hangs against the chin.

To make an attached mustache, use another chenille stem and shorter bundles of yarn. Secure the yarn bundles to the stem as for the beard. Twist the ends of the stem onto the top of the beard *(SEE DRAWING 37).*

CHAPTER 5

Shoes, Paws, Tails, and Claws

Costume pieces that fit over the feet and hands are not only fun for children to wear, but lend authenticity to dress-up situations. Since these are pieces that children may put on and take off repeatedly during the course of play, they have been designed with child-friendly attachments; with the exception of shoelaces and ties, children should be able to use them independently. Remember, when paws and other hand gear cover only the back of the hands, leaving the palms bare, they are much easier for children to manage. Such hand coverings let children try out "paws" or other appendages without hampering coordination and manual dexterity. Likewise, costume accessories for the feet can be constructed so that the bottoms of the shoes have direct contact with the floor, preventing slipping and loss of balance. When costume accessories do cover the palms and the soles, as with felt or mittens or gloves, use rubber cement to add grip and traction. Simply brush three or four lines or a grid of rubber cement on the bottom of socks, felt paws, and so on. When the rubber cement dries, it provides just enough resistance to help children move and manage comfortably in these fun costume additions.

From Nifty, Thrifty, No-Sew Costumes & Props published by Good Year Books. Copyright © 1998 Good Year Books.

Shoes, Boots, Paws, and Claws

Shoe Box Shoes/Boots/Feet
(DRAWING 38)

Basic Materials

- *shoe boxes*
- *felt*
- *glue*

Assembly:

1. Turn two shoe boxes upside-down and set the lids aside for other use.

2. Cut a hole in the bottoms of the boxes such that the child's stocking foot can fit inside the box. Or cut a larger hole and then glue a sheet of felt inside the box, covering the hole. Cut a hole in the felt such that the child's stocking foot can fit through the box. Children wear Shoe Box Shoes directly over their shoes. They likely will have to remove their shoes before stepping into Shoe Box Shoes, then put them back on under the shoe box.

Decorate:

- Use the tip of a pair of scissors or a hole punch to make several holes along both sides of the opening on the top of the box. Put yarn or ribbon "shoe laces" through the holes.

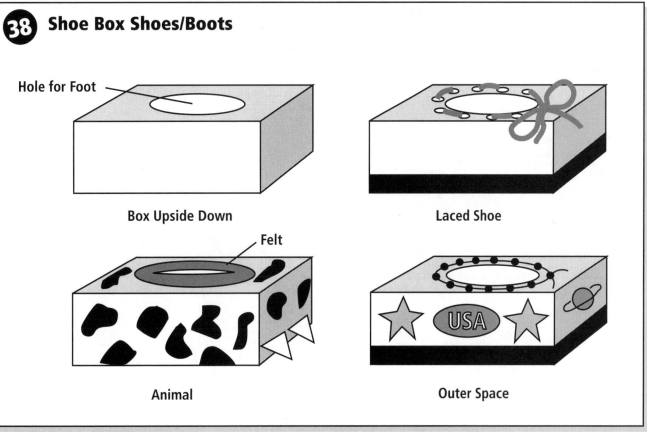

38 Shoe Box Shoes/Boots

Hole for Foot

Box Upside Down

Laced Shoe

Felt

Animal

Outer Space

USA

- Draw a "sole" around the bottom of the shoe (which is actually the top of the box) with markers, or cut felt strips for the sole and glue them on.

- Cover Shoe Box Shoes with construction paper, felt, or gift wrap. Or, try painting them.

- Embellish the shoes with felt or paper shapes, spots, or stripes. Attach with glue.

- **CLAWS ON SHOE BOX FEET:** Make claws/toenails for Animal Paws or Dinosaur Feet (see following) by cutting triangles out of polystyrene foam and gluing them to the top front ends of the shoe boxes. White felt triangles also work well as claws.

  (SEE DRAWING 38).

Variations:

- **SPACE BOOTS:** Spray paint Shoe Box Shoes with silver, or glue on aluminum foil. Attach wide strips of white felt around the bottom edge for boot soles. Glue foil or glitter stars to top or sides.

- **ANIMAL PAWS:** Cover shoe boxes with fake fur or fleece. Measure around the shoe box and cut one long piece of fur or fleece, or cut an individual piece for each side. Spread a generous amount of glue on the shoe box and attach the fake fur or fleece. Use spring clothespins to hold the fabric in place while it dries. Alternatively, simply paint boxes: gray for elephant feet, orange for duck feet, and green for frog feet. Add paper toenails as appropriate.

- **DINOSAUR FEET:** Paint shoe boxes green, brown, or yellow. Glue on felt spots if desired. Or, cover boxes with paper twist: untwist the paper twist and glue on wide strips, along the length of the sides and across the top of the box. Make spikes for Shoe Box Dinosaur Feet out of small paper cones and glue them on. To make claws see directions on above left.

Idea Starter

WHO'S IN THE ZOO? Make table cages to accompany animal costumes (or even one favorite animal tunic) for a pretend zoo. Wrap yarn or heavy cord horizontally around all four table legs, leaving a 2" space between the "bars." Children spread the yarn apart to get in and out of the cage. Add rugs, food bowls, and even stuffed animals to cages. Make a *Zoo* sign and individual signs to identify caged animals.

Paper Bag Boots/Shoes *(DRAWING 39)*

Basic Materials

- *medium-sized brown paper grocery bags*
- *hole punch*
- *masking tape*
- *yarn*

Assembly:

1. Cut the top third off of two medium-sized brown bags and set the tops aside for later use. For a shorter boot, cut the bags in half.

2. Punch holes 1" apart around the tops of the bags. Position the holes about 1"–2" from the top edge of the bags. To make the holes tear resistant, place a strip of masking tape around the top edge of the bag (on the inside) before punching holes.

3. Cut two 18" pieces of yarn and lace the yarn through the holes around each Paper Bag Boot. Pull on the yarn to tighten, gathering and pleating the bag around the leg. Leave the bottom of the bag on, or remove it so that Paper Bag Boots can be worn over shoes.

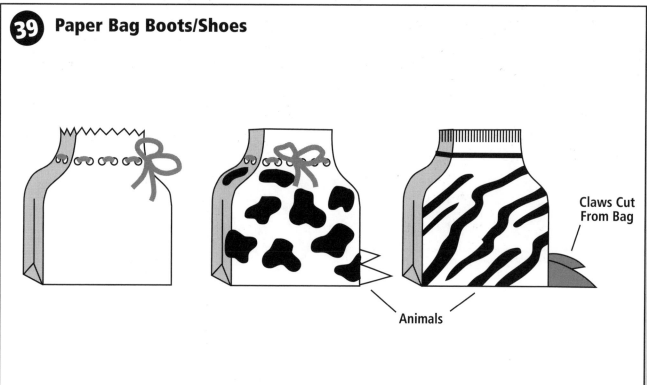

39 Paper Bag Boots/Shoes

Claws Cut
From Bag

Animals

- **CLAWS ON PAPER BAG FEET:** Cut out polystyrene foam or white felt triangle claws and glue them onto one side of the bag. Alternatively, cut claws directly out of one side of the bags. To do so, draw three or four triangles on the bag. Cut the two sides (but not the bottom) of the triangles, leaving them attached to the bag at the base. Bend the triangles out so that they look like claws protruding from the Paper Bag Animal Paws (SEE DRAWING 39).

Decorate:

- Use crayons, markers, or paint to color the boots.
- Cut paper or felt designs and attach them to the Paper Bag Boots with glue.

Variation:

- **ANIMAL PAWS:** Draw stripes, spots, scales, or fur on the bags with markers or crayons.

Felt Leg Coverings (Boot Tops)
(DRAWING 40)

Basic Materials

- *felt*
- *hole punch*
- *yarn, ribbon, or string*

Assembly:

1. Cut felt 10" × 8", 10", or 12", depending how high the Leg Coverings will be.

2. Punch holes at $\frac{1}{2}$" intervals on both sides of the 8", 10", or 12" edge.

3. Begin at the bottom of the Leg Covering and lace yarn, ribbon, or string through the holes in a crisscross pattern. Wear the Leg Coverings over pants, tights, or bare legs, placing ties at the side, front, or back of the leg.

40 **Felt Leg Coverings**

Holes

Decorate:

- Coordinate colors with characters and occupations depicted: black or gray for firefighters and miners, brown or tan for Western and sports costumes, green shades for elves and gnomes, and white for astronauts.

- Add yarn spirals, snakes, and curves, for a Western look.

- Add aluminum foil stars and crescents, for an outer-space look. Shapes cut from aluminum pie pans and baking pans also work well.

- Draw designs on Leg Coverings with fabric paint or acrylic paint.

Variations:

- Tie Leg Coverings close to the tops of the shoes to approximate low boots, and higher up on the leg for higher boots. Make Leg Coverings of different sizes to use as boots of different heights on the legs.

- Cut an extra 4" onto the length of the 10" or 12" Leg Coverings and fold the extra length down, like a boot top. Cut a fringe on the extra fold (SEE DRAWING 40).

Idea Starter

PARADE OF PAWS: Have an animal parade with children either in full costume or wearing only animal paws. Encourage growling, squawking, barking, and other animal noises. It's fun to position mirrors (9 x 12 or larger) on the floor so that children will see their feet as the Parade of Paws goes by.

Felt Shoes (DRAWING 41)

Basic Materials

- *felt*
- *hole punch*
- *yarn*
- *rubber cement*

Assembly:

1. Cut two pieces of felt about 3"–4" larger than the child's foot on all sides.

2. Cut slits or punch holes around the edge of the felt at 1" intervals. Place the holes $\frac{1}{2}$"–1" from the edge.

3. Lace an 18" piece of yarn through the holes.

4. Place several lines or a grid of rubber cement on the soles of the Felt Shoes and let dry. (This will provide some traction on bare floors.) Children wear Felt Shoes with only socks underneath. Have them place their foot in the center of the felt. Pull on both pieces of yarn, gathering the felt up around the foot, and tie. Trim the yarn ties so that they are not too long.

Decorate:

- Cut 1" felt shapes, such as circles, ovals, triangles, hearts, or stars, and attach them with fabric glue.

- Attach pompoms, tassels, and bows with glue, or punch two holes in the Felt Shoes and tie on the decorations with yarn.

- Use dimensional paint or fabric paint to decorate Felt Shoes.

- Lace ribbon instead of yarn through the holes in the shoes.

- Add bells or small beads and charms to yarn or ribbon ties. Position the bells or beads in the front, where the shoes tie, or attach them at each hole all the way around the shoes.

- Cut a decorative border on the edge of the felt, such as fringe, scallops, or zigzags.

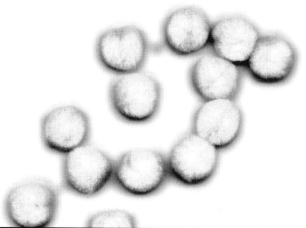

41 **Felt Shoes**

Shoe Top

From *Nifty, Thrifty, No-Sew Costumes & Props* published by Good Year Books. Copyright © 1998 Good Year Books.

Variations:

- **FELT BOOTS:** Cut the felt 6"–8" larger than the child's foot and then follow the Felt Shoes procedure.

- **FELT SHOE TOPS:** Cut shoe top from felt. Add holes and yarn ties on the side of each shoe so they can be tied around the ankles. Add laces or a felt buckle to decorate.

- **DIVER FINS:** Cut fins from felt. Add holes and yarn ties on the sides of each fin so that they can be tied around the ankles.

Sock Paws and Shoes (DRAWING 42)

Basic Materials

- *socks (adult sizes work best)*
- *rubber cement*

Assembly:

Cut most of the foot off of the socks, leaving intact only a middle section, like a stirrup, that will fit around the bottom of the foot. Or, leave the bottom intact and apply rubber cement (in a grid pattern or make several long lines) to the sole of the foot. (The rubber cement will provide traction on bare floors.) Wear Sock Paws directly over shoes or on stocking feet if Sock Paws fit tighter.

Decorate:

- Draw directly on the socks with markers, fabric paint, or dimensional paint. Make animal spots, stripes, scales, and feathers. Add toes, toenails, or claws. To make Sock Paws more realistic, outline colored features with a black marker.

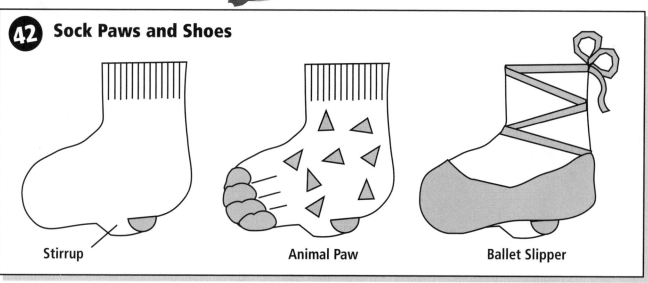

42 Sock Paws and Shoes

Stirrup   Animal Paw   Ballet Slipper

- Glue felt shapes onto Sock Paws: circles and ovals for spots or scales, narrow strips for stripes, triangles for claws, and half circles for toenails.

Variation:

- **BALLET SLIPPERS:** Use fabric paint to draw and color in the toe, heel, and sides of the sock to resemble a ballet slipper. Draw ribbon in a crisscross design from the foot to the top of the sock. Or, glue a 12" piece of ribbon in a crisscross pattern from the bottom to the top of the sock (SEE DRAWING 42).

- **BIRD LEGS:** Use fabric paint to draw and color in bird legs and feet. Then tie a felt bird foot (see directions on p. 79 for Felt Paws) around each ankle. Decorate the feet with glued on feathers.

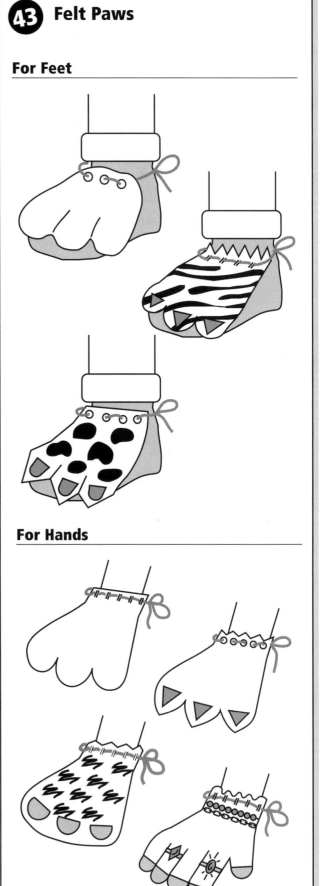

43 Felt Paws

For Feet

For Hands

Fancy Hand

From *Nifty, Thrifty, No-Sew Costumes & Props* published by Good Year Books. Copyright © 1998 Good Year Books.

Felt Paws *(DRAWING 43)*

Basic Materials

- *felt*
- *hole punch*
- *yarn*

Assembly:

1. Trace a paper pattern around the child's foot or hand, making it about 1" larger all the way around. Shape the pattern into an animal paw, bird claw, or dinosaur foot, for example. Use the paper pattern to cut two or four paws or feet from felt.

2. Punch a row of holes at 1" intervals across the top straight edge of the paw.

3. Lace an 8"–10" piece of yarn through the holes. Children wear Felt Paws, laying them on top of their hands or feet and tying them at the back of the wrist or ankle. Felt Paws can be worn on top of shoes, if desired.

Decorate:

- Cut spots, stripes, hooves, or scales from felt of another color and attach them to the Paws with glue.

- Draw features such as spots and stripes on the Paws with dimensional paint.

- Make a fringe or a zigzag cut all the way around the Paws to suggest animal fur.

- **CLAWS ON FELT PAWS:** Attach white felt or polystyrene foam claws to the end of the Paws with glue.

Variations:

- **BIRD FEET/WINGS:** Attach feathers all over the Felt Feet and Hands to accompany a bird costume. Use fabric glue to attach either real feathers or feathers made out of felt.

- **CARDBOARD PAWS:** Use poster board in the same way to make paws that tie on feet or hands. Decorate with paint or felt spots and strips. Add claws as desired.

- **FURRY PAWS:** Cut paws from fake fur or fleece. Attach felt claws and tie the Fur Paws on the hands and feet.

- **FANCY HANDS:** Cut hand shapes from skin-tone felt colors (white, pink, orange, tan, brown, or black). Attach felt "polished" fingernails, and glue on beads, sequins, or glitter jewelry, such as rings and bracelets. Use ribbon instead of yarn to tie on Fancy Hands *(SEE DRAWING 43)*.

Glove and Mitten Paws/Hands

(DRAWING 44)

Basic Materials

- *a pair of gloves or mittens (plain colors work best)*
- *glue*

Assembly:

The only assembly required for these Paws is the addition of items to the gloves or mittens that relate them to a particular animal or character. Choose mittens in colors that correspond to the animal or character being depicted, or use white gloves or mittens and various colors of fabric paint. Decorate the tops only, leaving the palms plain. Apply rubber cement to the palms of the gloves or mittens, if desired.

Decorate:

- **BIRDS:** Add feathers or felt ovals to gloves or mittens, to suggest wing tips.

- **SNAKES OR DINOSAURS:** Use fabric paint to draw scales on mittens. Or, glue on felt petal shapes in an overlapping pattern. Begin at the fingertip of the mitten and work down, one row at a time. Glue the edge of the felt "scale" only, leaving the rounded end unglued. Attach a second row of "scales," gluing the edges only and positioning the scales so that they overlap those in the first row. Attach each row the same way, alternating the placement so that every other row matches.

- **ANIMALS:** Attach items that suggest animals, either real or pretend. Try felt spots or stripes, rows of pompoms, yarn stripes, or balls of cotton.

- **CLAWS ON PAWS:** Cut white felt triangles and glue them to the glove or mitten fingertips.

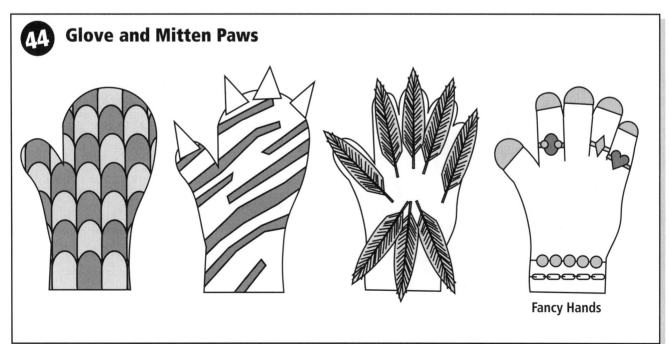

44 **Glove and Mitten Paws**

Fancy Hands

Variations:

- **FURRY PAWS:** Cut fake fur into small pieces that fit the glove or mitten and glue on cut strips to fit the fingers and a square with rounded corners to fit the back of the hand.

- **FANCY HANDS:** Use gloves in skin-tone colors and glue on pink or red felt or use pink or red fabric paint to "polish" fingernails. Add glitter, sequins, foil scraps, beads, and plastic gems as rings on fingers and as bracelets on wrists.

Tails

Having seen them on many animals that they play with and read about, tails are enormously fun for children to wear. To have a tail is to feel more like an animal, move like an animal, be an animal. Tails should be comfortable to wear and not limit movement. Long tails, while certainly fun for children to wear, must not be so long that they get in the way.

A variety of techniques can be used to attach tails comfortably and quickly. One of the easiest methods is to fasten a piece of yarn to any tail so that the tail can be secured to a belt, sash, or scarf. Simply tie the yarn onto the tail and knot the ends into a loop. Slide the loop onto any belt, felt sash, or scarf worn around the waist. Adjust the position of the tail by varying the size of the loop: to make a low-hanging tail, use a larger loop; for a shorter tail, make the loop smaller.

Tails can also be attached without the use of loops in the following ways:

- **BELTS:** Tie the tails securely to the middle of the belt with yarn or heavy string. Children wear the belt around the waist with the tail hanging down the back.

- **FELT SASH:** Attach a tail to a strip of felt 2" wide and 20"–24" long. Fasten the tail to the middle of the sash with yarn or string. Tie the felt band around the waist in the front or on the side, with the tail positioned in the back.

- **SCARVES:** Tie the tail onto a scarf that has been gathered up or folded lengthwise. Tie scarves around the waist so that the tail hangs down in the back. A scarf will be more secure and more comfortable than a piece of yarn or string.

Poster Board Tails *(DRAWING 45)*

Basic Materials

- *poster board, lightweight cardboard, or heavy paper*
- *hole punch*
- *yarn*

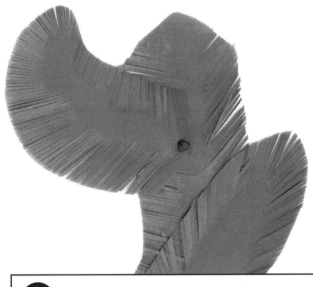

Assembly:

1. Use a pattern to make a tail or design one of your own. Trace the tail onto poster board and cut it out.

2. Punch a hole in the top of the tail.

3. Tie a 3"–4" loop of yarn through the hole. Use the loop to attach the tail to a belt, sash, or scarf.

Decorate:

- Use markers or paint to draw stripes, spots, and other features on the tail.

- Cut out construction paper features and glue them on the tail.

- Glue a yarn border around the edge of the tail.

- Glue yarn zigzags, straight lines, circles, spirals, or fringes on the tail.

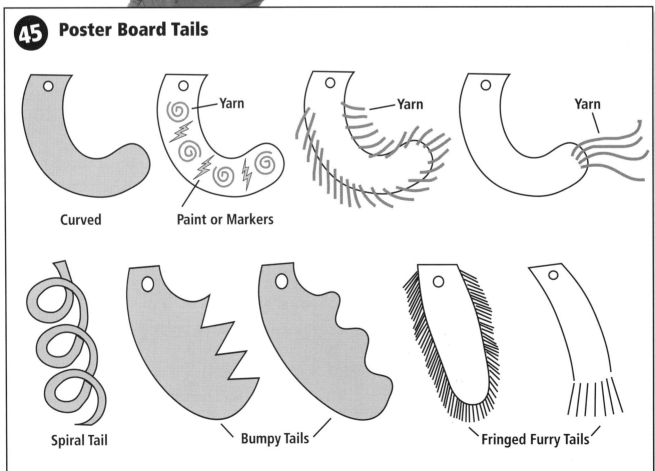

45 Poster Board Tails

Curved

Yarn — Paint or Markers

Yarn

Yarn

Spiral Tail

Bumpy Tails

Fringed Furry Tails

From *Nifty, Thrifty, No-Sew Costumes & Props* published by Good Year Books. Copyright © 1998 Good Year Books.

- Add six to eight 6" pieces of yarn to the tip of the tail, tying the pieces together in a bunch and attaching with glue.

- Punch holes around the outer edge of the tail. Cut 6" lengths of yarn and tie one or two in each hole, for a fringed, furry tail.

- Glue pompoms on the tail. Use craft pompoms or make pompoms with yarn (p. 102).

- Cut ovals, circles, zigzags, and other shapes from materials that add interest, texture, and dimension to tails: cotton, sandpaper, felt, fake fur, fleece, and burlap.

- Glue feathers on tails. Use craft feathers or make feathers out of felt (p. 103).

Variations:

- **SPIRAL TAIL:** Cut a 12"–14" diameter circle of poster board. Begin cutting at one edge of the circle and cut in a spiral motion toward the center without cutting off any of the circle. This will make a curly, spiraling tail. For a smaller spiral tail, cut a smaller circle.

- **BUMPY TAIL:** Make a 1'–3' tail, cutting spikes, bumps, scallops, or zigzags along the edges.

- **FURRY TAIL:** Cut a tail of the desired shape and size, then fringe the edges. Fringe all three sides or just the tip of the tail.

Felt Tails (DRAWING 46)

Basic Materials

- *felt*
- *hole punch*
- *yarn*

Assembly:

1. Use a pattern to make a tail or design one of your own. Trace onto felt and cut out.

2. Punch a hole in the top of the tail and tie a loop of yarn through it, for attachment purposes.

46 Felt Tails

Decorate:

- Use a dark-colored permanent marker or fabric paint to draw spots, stripes, scales, or feathers on the tail. Add a border with paint or markers.

- Cut shapes from felt and glue them to the Felt Tail. Try circles, ovals, narrow strips, and zigzags.

- Glue yarn, pompoms, or craft feathers to the tail.

Variations:

- Make Spiral, Bumpy, or Furry Tails using the Poster Board Tail techniques. Or, try making a Forked Tail, as for a fish.

- For added dimension and realism, use fabric glue to attach chenille stems to the underside of the tail. Apply a line of glue down the center of the tail. Place several chenille stems end to end on the glue. Press firmly and let the stems dry. With the addition of chenille stems, tails can be bent and formed in a variety of ways.

Paper Twist Tails *(DRAWING 47)*

Basic Materials

- *paper twist*
- *hole punch*
- *yarn*

Assembly:

1. Cut a 1'–3' length of paper twist.

2. Untwist the paper twist and fold one end under several times to make it sturdier.

3. Punch a hole in the folded end of the tail and put a loop of yarn through it for attachment purposes.

Decorate:

- Add several strands of yarn to the end of the Paper Twist Tail.

- Use markers to draw features on the tail.

Variations:

- Make a thin tail with a length of paper twist that has not been untwisted.

- Keep the top of the tail twisted but untwist the bottom 6"–10" of the tail *(SEE DRAWING 47).*

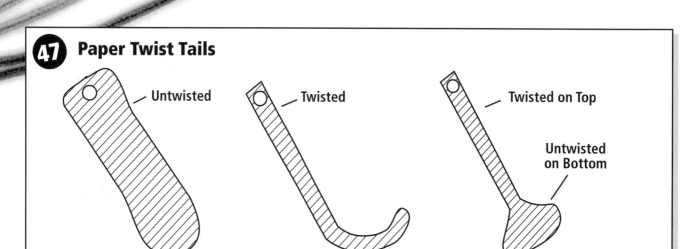

47 Paper Twist Tails

Untwisted

Twisted

Twisted on Top

Untwisted on Bottom

Sock Tails *(DRAWING 48)*

MATERIALS

- socks *(adult size)*
- stuffing material: cotton, shredded paper, fiberfill
- yarn

Assembly:

1. Fill a sock with a stuffing material.

2. Tie off the top of the sock and add a loop of yarn for attachment.

Decorate:

- Add details to the Sock Tail with markers or dimensional paint.

- Attach a yarn tassel to the end of the tail.

- Cut felt shapes to represent spots, stripes, and other features. Glue them to the Sock Tail.

Variations:

- **STRAIGHT TAIL:** To eliminate a curve at the bottom of the tail, use a tube sock or remove about half of the foot section of a standard sock. Stuff and tie both ends.

- **SMALL/SHORT TAIL:** To make a shorter, smaller tail, stuff a child's sock or cut an adult's sock down to size.

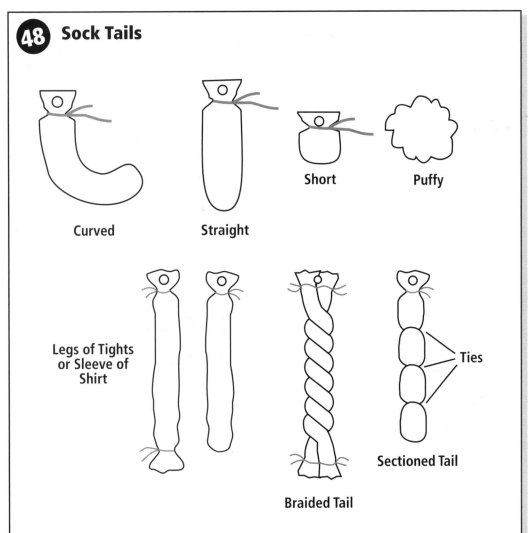

48 Sock Tails

Curved

Straight

Short

Puffy

Legs of Tights or Sleeve of Shirt

Braided Tail

Sectioned Tail

Ties

- **PUFFY TAIL:** Stuff the middle of a sock loosely and tie the toe to the top. Form the sock into a rounder, softer tail, as for a rabbit.

- **STOCKING TAIL:** Remove one leg from a pair of tights or opaque stockings. Cut off the foot section and tie off the end. Stuff the leg and tie off the other end. Turn the stocking inside out before stuffing, for a rounded, smooth end, or keep the stocking as is, for a tail with a "tassel" of fabric at the end.

- **SLEEVE TAIL:** The sleeves from a worn-out sweatshirt make fun tails and offer a wide range of color choices. Remove the sleeves and tie the cuffed ends with yarn. Stuff each sleeve and tie the top with yarn. Turn the sleeve inside out before stuffing, for a soft, fleece tail, or leave as is, for a smoother tail. For a narrow tail, fold the sleeve in half before stuffing and secure between the fold with fabric glue. Stuff and trim.

- **DINOSAUR SLEEVE TAIL:** Attach several felt triangles to the seam of the sleeve with fabric glue. Place glue on one edge of the triangles so that they will stand up.

- **BRAIDED TAIL:** Stuff two legs loosely, following the directions for the Stocking Tail. Tie the two together at one end with yarn, and "braid" (twist) the stocking lengths. Tie the other end with yarn *(SEE DRAWING 48).*

- **SECTIONED TAIL:** Make a Sock Tail, Stocking Tail, or Sleeve Tail and stuff it lightly rather than firmly. Use 8" pieces of yarn to tie around the tails in three or four sections. Wrap the yarn around twice and pull tightly before tying, to make a tail that is divided, or jointed, in several sections *(SEE DRAWING 48).*

Yarn and Rope Tails *(DRAWING 49)*

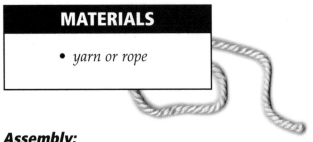

MATERIALS
• *yarn or rope*

Assembly:

1. Cut nine pieces of yarn or rope, each 32" long.

2. Wrap a shorter piece of yarn several times around the middle and knot it. The tied middle section becomes the top of the tail. The bottom of the tail consists of eighteen pieces of yarn, each 16" long.

3. Tie a loop of yarn on the top for attachment.

Make longer or shorter tails by adjusting the lengths of the yarn cut.

Decorate:

- Tie a ribbon or several brightly colored strands of yarn around the tail, placing it 3"–5" from the top.

Variations:

- **BRAIDED TAIL:** Divide the eighteen pieces of yarn into three equal sections, six pieces per section. Braid the sections together, making a thick Braided Tail. If you wish, try further dividing the yarn into three sections of two strands per section. Braid the sections together, for a Braided Tail that consists of nine thin braids.

- **BEADED TAIL:** String several large wooden beads on about half of the yarn pieces in the tail. Position the beads randomly along the yarn, tying a knot under each to keep it in place.

- **KNOTTED TAIL:** Group the yarn into three sections, six strands per section. Tie several knots in each section. Position the knots randomly along the top, middle, and end of the strands.

- **FABRIC STRIP TAIL:** Tear or cut (regular shears or pinking shears) 1" strips of fabric in a variety of lengths, from 16" to 30". Use one color or print per tail or mix colors and prints together. Wrap a piece of yarn around the middle of the fabric strips and tie tightly. The tied middle becomes the top of the tail; the remainder will consist of 8"–15" long strips.

- **CLOTHESLINE, HEAVY STRING, JUTE, OR RAFFIA TAIL:** To make these fun-to-wear tails, follow the same basic procedures.

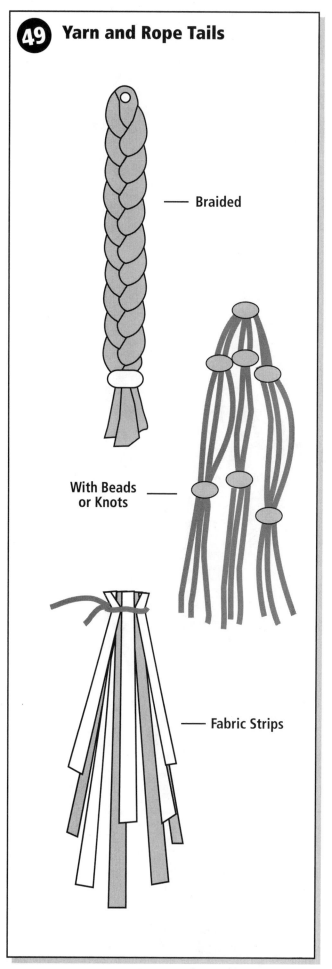

49 Yarn and Rope Tails

— Braided

With Beads or Knots —

— Fabric Strips

Antennas, Crests, Antlers, Fins, and All the Rest

From a safety standpoint, full face masks are not a practical choice for dress-up play. They can be restrictive and uncomfortable for many children to use. The headbands and forehead bands described in this section make an excellent alternative. These costume pieces can be decorated to suggest everything from animals, insects, birds, and fish to dinosaurs, monsters, and space creatures, without covering the face.

From *Nifty, Thrifty, No-Sew Costumes & Props* published by Good Year Books. Copyright © 1998 Good Year Books.

Idea Starter

INSECT GARDEN: Create a garden for children to use when they wear insect costumes (See Bumblebee, p. 177). Tape together large pieces of posterboard or paint several pieces of newsprint green and place them on the floor in a corner. Use yarn and construction paper to create oversized vines, leaves, and flowers (p. 117) to create a "larger than life" paper garden. Insect-costumed children will feel like tiny bugs in a big world!

Antennas *(DRAWING 50)*

Use Antennas for insects of all kinds, including bumblebees and butterflies, and for space creatures.

Basic Materials

- *headband*
- *chenille stems*
- *polystyrene foam balls*
- *glue*

Assembly:

1. Use the point of a pencil to poke a hole in two polystyrene foam balls.

2. Put glue and a chenille stem in each ball.

3. Wrap the ends of the chenille stems around a headband, attaching them to the top of the band, about 3"–4" apart.

Decorate:

- Cover polystyrene foam balls with glitter, paint, or tufts of tissue paper before gluing them on the ends of the chenille stems.

Variations:

- Attach two balls of crumpled paper or foil the same way.

- Use pompoms on the ends of the chenille stems.

- Coil the chenille stems to look like a spring by wrapping one end around a pencil. Twist two chenille stems together for a longer coil.

- Cut two small spirals from construction paper of a contrasting color. To make a spiral, begin with a 2" diameter circle. Cut into the circle and continue cutting around the circle to the center without removing any of the circle. Poke a hole in each end of the spirals and thread one end onto the chenille stem. Loosely wind the paper spiral around the stem from top to bottom, then attach the second hole.

- Use four stems instead of two. Attach a ball on the end of each and position on the headband at different heights.

- **BAND HAT ANTENNAS:** Attach antennas to Band Hats (p. 34), such as those made for insects, space aliens, or robots. Staple or glue antennas to inside of band. Cover the sharp side of the staple with tape.

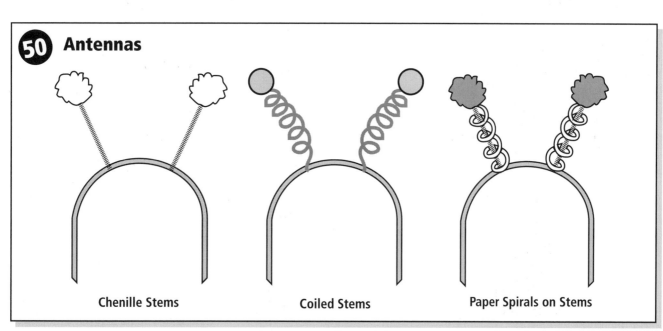

50 **Antennas**

Chenille Stems   Coiled Stems   Paper Spirals on Stems

Plumes and Crests *(DRAWING 51)*

Use these head pieces for insects, birds, and dinosaurs.

Basic Materials

- *construction paper*
- *hole punch*
- *brass fasteners*
- *stapler*

Assembly:

1. Cut a 2" × 20"–24" forehead band from construction paper.

2. Punch several holes in one end and one hole in the other so that the band can be adjusted to fit the child's head. Attach with brass fasteners.

3. Cut a half circle with a 6" diameter from construction paper.

4. Fanfold the half circle and staple it to the front center of the forehead band.

Decorate:

- Cover the half circle with brightly colored gift wrap or foil before folding and attaching.

- Cut the edge with scallops or zigzags.

- Cut a fringe on the rounded edge of the Crest.

- Attach feathers to the Crest with glue. Attach feathers directly to the forehead band, across the front and back. Position the feathers in all directions: sideways, upward, downward, and slanted.

- Make tufts of tissue paper and glue them randomly all over the Crest.

Variations:

- Use half of a paper plate instead of construction paper. Fanfold the plate, attach to the front center of the forehead band, and decorate.

- Cut a large plastic coffee can lid in half and decorate one side with feathers, pompoms, or tufts of tissue paper. Attach it to the front center of the forehead band with a stapler. To help objects adhere to the plastic lid, rough up the lid with sandpaper before applying glue.

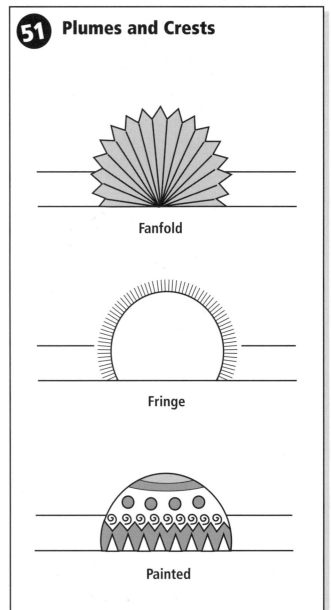

51 Plumes and Crests

Fanfold

Fringe

Painted

Antlers and Horns *(DRAWING 52)*

Use Antlers and Horns on animals of all kinds, including dinosaurs and monsters.

Basic Materials

- *construction paper*
- *paper towel tube*
- *glue*
- *stapler or tape*
- *hole punch*
- *brass fasteners*

Antlers

Assembly:

1. Cut a 2" × 20"–24" strip of construction paper.

2. Punch several holes in one end and one hole in the other so that the band can be adjusted to fit the child's head. Attach with brass fasteners.

3. Trace the child's hands onto cardboard and cut them out. Do the same on a piece of construction paper.

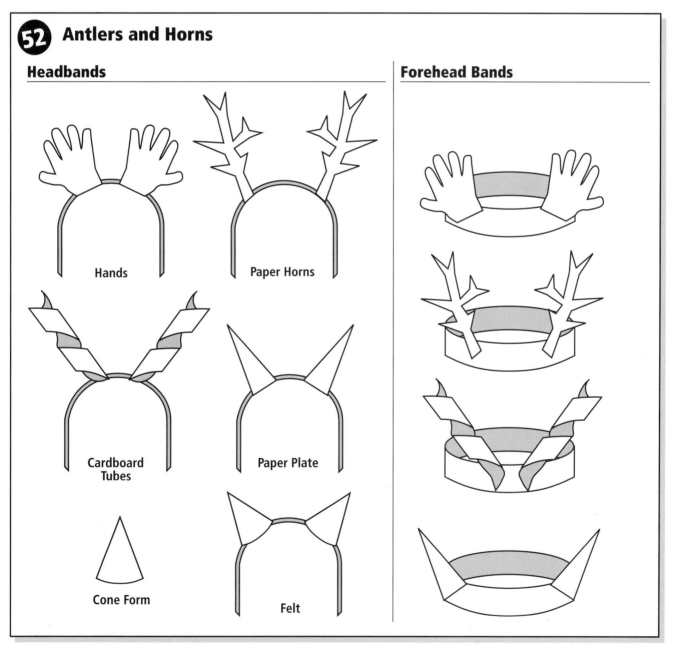

52 **Antlers and Horns**

Headbands

Hands

Paper Horns

Cardboard Tubes

Paper Plate

Cone Form

Felt

Forehead Bands

4. Glue the construction paper hands onto the cardboard hands.

5. Attach the hands on either side of the forehead band, to make very personal Antlers, each as unique as the hands themselves. Use tape or a stapler to attach Antlers.

Variations:

■ **FELT ANTLERS:** Cut the second set of hands out of felt and glue them onto cardboard before attaching to the forehead band.

■ **BENDABLE ANTLERS:** Cut two sets of hands from felt. Glue sections of chenille stem between the felt hands, positioning one along each finger and one or two on the palms. Let dry. Attach the Felt Antlers to the forehead band with a stapler. The chenille stems will not be visible, yet will allow the antlers to be bent and shaped.

■ **PAPER BAG ANTLERS:** Cut the second set of hands out of a brown paper grocery bag. Crumple the paper bag hands and smooth them back out a bit. Paint the bag hands with a watered-down paint. (The wrinkles on the paper will absorb more paint and create a more realistic look.) Glue the Paper Bag Antlers onto the cardboard and attach them on the forehead band. Alternatively, coat the crumpled antlers with several applications of sealer (such as Plaid® Mod Podge or Delta® Sobo Glue). The sealer will make the Antlers sturdier and eliminate the need for a cardboard backing.

■ **BRANCH ANTLERS:** Gather together thin tree branches, about 5"–6" in length. Tape the branches to the outside of the forehead band, for a very natural pair of antlers.

■ **HEADBAND ANTLERS:** Attach Paper, Cardboard, Paper Bag, or Felt Antlers on the top of a plastic headband with tape for Antlers that are worn on top of the head. These temporary Antlers can be removed and changed as needed.

Idea Starter

AN OCEAN OF FISH: Use the same idea as the Insect Garden Idea Starter (p. 88) to create an ocean atmosphere for Fish (p. 183), Mermaids (p. 186), and Divers (p. 180). Begin with brown or yellow poster board or painted newsprint as the sandy ocean floor. Use crepe paper, construction paper, and cellophane to make seaweed, waves, seashells, fish, and other sea creatures.

Horns

Basic Materials

- *construction paper*
- *poster board or light-weight cardboard*
- *glue*
- *hole punch*
- *brass fasteners*
- *tape or stapler*

Assembly:

1. Cut a 2" × 20"–24" strip of construction paper.

2. Punch several holes in one end and one hole in the other so that the band can be adjusted to fit the child's head. Attach with brass fasteners.

3. Cut a cardboard paper towel tube in half. Pull or cut each section of the tube in half on the diagonal.

4. Cover both sides of the tube sections with an appropriate color of construction paper or use uncovered. Attach the paper with glue.

5. Staple or tape one end of each tube to either side of the forehead band.

Variations:

- **FELT HORNS:** Cover the two tube sections with felt, either on one side or both sides, before attaching to the forehead band.

- **PAPER PLATE HORNS:** Cut a 8"–9" diameter paper plate in half. Cover both halves with paper or felt, or leave plain. Roll both pieces into a cone and tape the edges. Trim the end and remove any excess paper from the inside of the cone. Attach the Paper Plate Horns to either side of the forehead band with a stapler.

- **POLYSTYRENE FOAM HORNS:** Trace a pattern for two horns onto polystyrene foam food trays and cut them out. Glue or tape the horns onto either side of the forehead band.

- **CARDBOARD HORNS:** Follow the procedure for the Polystyrene Foam Horns, using poster board or lightweight cardboard instead. Try decorating with paint.

- **FABRIC HORNS:** Cut a 6"–8" diameter circle of cardboard. Slit the circle from the edge to the center and roll into a cone, taping the edges. Trim the bottom so that the cone sits flat. Cover the cardboard cone with waxed paper, tucking the ends of the paper under the bottom of the cone. Cut a 6"–8" diameter circle of burlap or other sturdy fabric. Again, slit from the edge to the center. Soak the fabric in liquid starch or a fabric stiffener. Squeeze out the excess liquid and form the fabric over the cardboard/waxed paper cone. Overlap the edges and trim the excess fabric from the bottom. Let the fabric dry completely, then loosen it from the cardboard form. Peel off any waxed paper that adheres to the fabric. Make two Fabric Cones this way, and staple them to either side of the forehead band.

- **HEADBAND HORNS:** Attach Paper Towel Tube, Paper Plate, Felt, or Cardboard Horns to the top of a plastic headband with tape. Remove and change them as needed.

Fins (DRAWING 53)

Use the fin accessories for fish and other underwater life.

Basic Materials

- *construction paper*
- *polystyrene foam food trays*
- *poster board or lightweight cardboard*
- *hole punch*
- *brass fasteners*
- *acrylic paint*
- *paintbrush*
- *sandpaper*

Assembly:

1. Cut a 2" × 20"–24" strip of construction paper. Punch several holes in one end and one hole in the other so that the band can be adjusted to fit the child's head. Attach with brass fasteners.

2. Trace a traditional fin design or one of your own onto cardboard. Cut out the fins and use them as patterns for polystyrene foam fins.

3. Make a variety of polystyrene foam fins. Cut out the fins.

4. Use a blunt instrument, such as a craft stick or the end of a paintbrush, to draw details on the fins, pressing into, but not through, the polystyrene foam. Draw shapes, lines, dots, and zigzags.

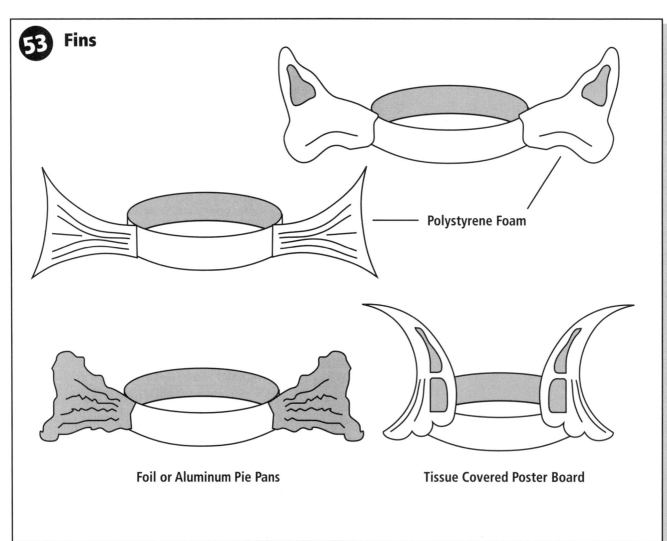

53 Fins

Polystyrene Foam

Foil or Aluminum Pie Pans

Tissue Covered Poster Board

5. Paint the fins with acrylic paint, making sure that the paint penetrates the designed area more heavily. When the paint dries, these areas will appear darker and lend a more realistic look. To help paint adhere to polystyrene foam, lightly sand before painting.

6. Attach fins to the forehead band in a variety of positions: front, side, back, or all the way around the band. Try attaching two or more different shapes to each side and positioning the fins on a slant, facing up or down.

Decorations

■ For a wet look, tape cellophane around the polystyrene foam fins.

■ Glue on eyes, either made from construction paper or felt, or purchase wiggle eyes from a craft store.

Variations:

■ **SHINY FINS:** Follow the procedure for making polystyrene foam fins, using aluminum pie pans instead. Put tape around the edges if they seem sharp or unevenly cut. Decorate Shiny Fins with colored tape, paper scraps, and stickers. Glitter also works well.

■ **TISSUE PAPER FINS:** Follow the procedure for making polystyrene foam fins, using cardboard or poster board as a base. Tear colored tissue paper into pieces of various sizes and shapes. Using a brush, coat the fins with a glue and water mixture (3 parts glue to 1 part water). Lay the tissue paper on top of the glued cardboard, overlapping it to create a colorful scale look.

Tentacles, Claws, and Pincers
(DRAWING 54)

Combine Tentacles, Claws, and Pincers, with other features, such as antennas and eyes.

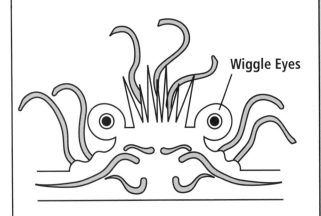

Tentacles

Cut thin 4"–8" lengths of cardboard. Cut some pieces straight and curve others. Round the ends of the pieces. Use markers or paint to color the Tentacles, or cover them with construction paper before cutting. Attach four to six Tentacles to each side of a forehead band with tape or glue. For an interesting variation, cut the Tentacles out of felt and glue a chenille stem to one side of the felt. Attach Felt Tentacles to the forehead band and curve as desired.

Claws and Pinchers

Cut crab or lobster claws and insect pinchers out of poster board or polystyrene foam. Color with markers or paint. Tape or glue these features onto the sides of a forehead band.

Insect Bands *(DRAWING 55)*

Create the representation of any insect, real or pretend, on a forehead band. Instead of cutting the band in one long strip and adding the features separately, cut the features for the insect directly into the band, similar to the Eye Bands (p. 55). Add features such as antennas, eyes, feelers, legs, stingers, and pincers. Study photographs of insects for more ideas. Use materials such as chenille stems (straight or curled), egg carton sections, wiggle eyes, pompoms, large buttons, and fanfolded paper strips.

Insects

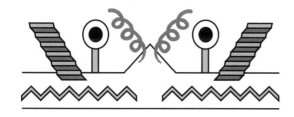

Plastic Rings

Birds

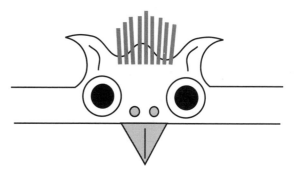

Space Aliens or Monsters

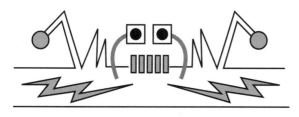

Insect Plastic Rings *(DRAWING 55)*

Cut two adjoining plastic six-pack rings, similar to the Plastic Ring Eyes (p. 57). Trace the rings onto felt or construction paper and cut them out. Glue the felt or paper rings on top of the plastic ones. Punch a hole in both sides of the rings and add yarn so that the Insect Rings can be tied behind the head. Wrap two chenille stems around the rings, either above the eyes or on the sides. Attach a pompom, flat felt circle, or crumpled ball of paper or foil to each stem, as antennas. If desired, attach a paper or felt diamond or triangle where the rings adjoin, so that it covers the child's nose. Crease these shapes before attaching, to add more dimension.

Space Alien and Monster Bands

(DRAWING 55)

Anything goes with these costume pieces! Use glue to attach paper spirals, chenille stems bent into any shape, pompoms, yarn, polystyrene foam pieces, and sections of paper towel tubes. Fasten paper and polystyrene foam pieces with brass fasteners so that they can be turned. Place wiggle eyes on the ends of chenille stems. Add antennas, claws, and other unusual features to these forehead bands. Be inventive when choosing and attaching items!

CHAPTER

7

Fairy Wings and Decorative Things: Wearable Props

Like props for hand-held use, the subject of the next chapter, wearable props are essential to imaginative dress-up play. Even a very simple costume will satisfy children and meet the needs of pretend play if an assortment of interesting wearable props are available. Many such props can be attached directly on tunics, collars, vests, and hats, creating a variety of looks from one basic costume or hat design. Make attachments permanent by gluing them on dress-up clothes, or fasten them temporarily, just for the day, by using any of the techniques discussed on page 33.

Belts *(DRAWING 56)*

Cut a felt strip 2" × 20". Punch a hole in each end of the strip. Cut a $2\frac{1}{2}$" × $3\frac{1}{2}$" oval or rectangle buckle from poster board. Add a bar in the center of the buckle. Cover the buckle with felt, attaching it with glue. Attach the buckle to the felt strip by threading the strip up through the buckle, over the bar, and down the other side. Holes can be placed in the belt, on one or both sides of the buckle. Place a plastic twist tie fastener through the hole so that keys, tools, and other items can be hung on the belt.

Variation:

- **ROBOT BELT:** Cut a 4" × 18"–20" strip of gray felt. Place one hole in each end. Thread an 8" piece of yarn through each hole and knot to make a tie for around the waist. Decorate the middle of the strip with a variety of felt shapes. Glue some shapes directly on the felt belt and attach others with brass fasteners so that they will turn like dials or knobs. Attach a row of plain brass fasteners across 4"–6" of the top and bottom of the belt. You can use yarn and felt to add a detachable "radio" or "speaker" to the belt similar to the one pictured on the Robot collar.

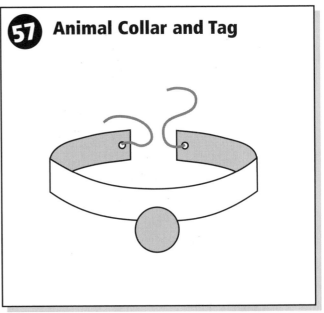

Animal Collar and Tag *(DRAWING 57)*

Cut a 2" × 16" strip of felt. Attach a 1" diameter circle of felt to the middle of the strip with glue for the tag. Punch a hole in each end of the strip and tie yarn through both sides so that the collar can be tied around the neck.

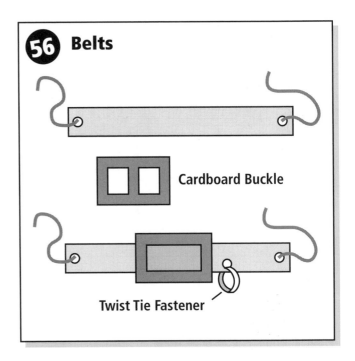

56 Belts

Cardboard Buckle

Twist Tie Fastener

57 Animal Collar and Tag

Idea Starter

HOCUS POCUS! MAGIC SHOW: Add the Wizard costume (p. 190) or just the hat and cape to props such as Wands (p. 134), Scepter (p. 133), Pouches (p. 123), and Crystal Balls (p. 134) to create a Magic Show atmosphere. Construct or gather other props such as a Brimmed Hat (p. 42), a felt rabbit, Paper Flowers (p. 117), paper birds, and several lengths of rope. A Stage (p. 25) and some music will add to the fun.

Neckties and Bow Ties *(DRAWING 58)*

Cut an 8"–10" tie shape from felt. Use a variety of colors. Decorate the Ties with contrasting colors of felt: dots, stripes, stars, crescents, hearts, diamonds, or any other shape. Attach the felt shapes with fabric glue.

Felt Ties can also be decorated with fabric paint or dimensional paint. Make Bow Ties by cutting a bow tie shape from felt and decorating it as for neckties. Fasten Neckties and Bow Ties to collars and tunic costumes either permanently or temporarily. Try punching two holes in the top of the ties and threading yarn through them so that Felt Neckties and Bow Ties can be tied around the neck.

58 Neckties and Bow Ties

Eye Patch

Make a cardboard pattern by tracing around one lens section of a pair of eyeglasses or sunglasses. Use the pattern to cut an eye patch from black felt. Place a hole in each of the two top corners of the felt piece. Lace a 36" piece of black yarn through both holes. To wear the eye patch, position the patch over the eye and tie the yarn around the head.

Bows *(DRAWING 59)*

Cut a piece of ribbon of any length (the size of the bow needed will dictate the length of ribbon to be cut). Tape the two ends of the ribbon together to form an oval. Tightly tie a piece of yarn in the center of the ribbon oval, bunching it into a Bow. Let the yarn ends hang free. A Bow can also be made with a 3"–6" length of paper twist. Simply wrap a chenille stem around the center of the paper twist. Untwist the paper on both sides of the chenille stem, fanning out the paper twist to form a Bow.

Pompoms *(DRAWING 60)*

Cut a 3" × 5" piece of cardboard. Lay a 10" piece of yarn along the 5" side and, holding this piece of yarn in place, wrap a second piece of yarn around the 3" width of the cardboard. Use enough yarn to cover the entire piece of cardboard this way, making two or three layers. After wrapping the yarn, tie the 10" piece as tightly as possible, pulling the wrapped yarn into a bunch. Cut through the yarn on the 5" side, opposite the tied 10" piece. Tighten the knot and fluff out the Pompom. Use the yarn ends to attach the Pompom to costumes, hats, shoes, and other dress-up pieces. Make Pompoms all one color or use several colors of yarn on one Pompom.

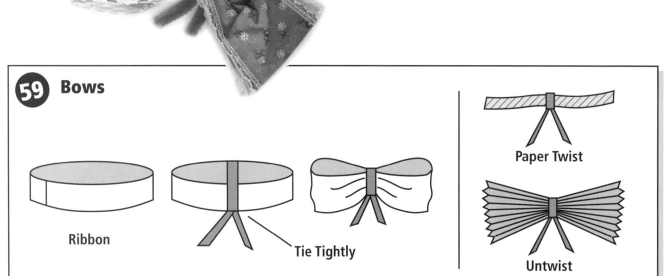

59 Bows

Ribbon

Tie Tightly

Paper Twist

Untwist

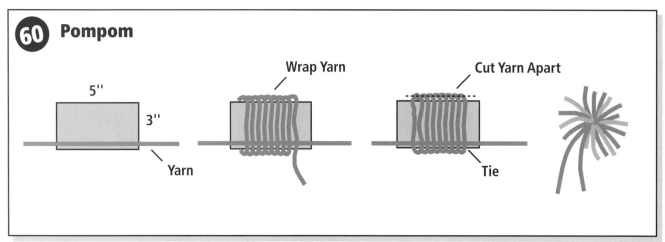

60 Pompom

5"

3"

Yarn

Wrap Yarn

Cut Yarn Apart

Tie

Variation:

- **TULLE POMPOM:** Fanfold a 6" x 24" piece of tulle, or use any length of tulle scrap remaining from making a Tulle Skirt (p. 28). Tie a 6" piece of yarn around the center of the folded tulle. Fluff out the tulle and use the yarn to attach the tulle pompom to the center of a 36" piece of wide satin ribbon. Use the ribbon to tie the tulle pompom around the hair, head, or waistband.

Tassels *(DRAWING 61)*

Follow the directions for making a Pompom, except lay the 10" tying yarn along the 3" side of the cardboard and wrap one layer only of yarn around the 5" side of the cardboard. Tie the 10" piece as tightly as possible, pulling the wrapped yarn in a bunch. Cut through the yarn on the 3" side, opposite the tied 10" piece. After cutting the yarn off the cardboard, tighten the knot, smooth the pieces in one direction, and tie a small piece of yarn around the Tassel, about 1" from the top. Use the 10" piece to tie the Tassel onto costumes and accessories.

Feathers *(DRAWING 62)*

Cut feather shapes from felt, varying color and sizes. Fringe the two sides of the feather by making small cuts into the felt. Attach a chenille stem to the back of the Felt Feather by running a line of glue down the center of the Feather. Press the chenille stem onto the glue and let dry. Once dry, the feather can be curved and bent. It will also stand erect when fastened on a hat or forehead band.

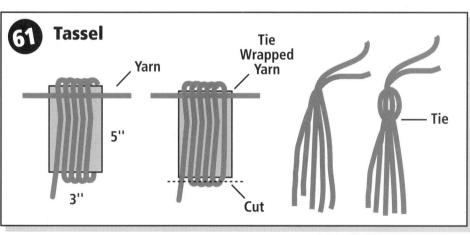

61 **Tassel**

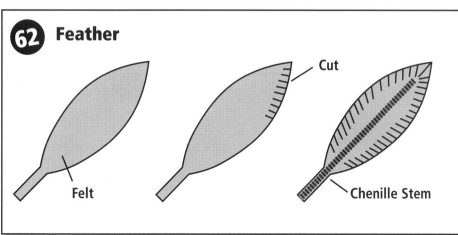

62 **Feather**

Rings *(DRAWING 63)*

CHENILLE STEM RING: Twist a 2"–3" piece of chenille stem once, at the point where it fits the finger. Twist the stem a second time, connecting the ends to form an oval or a circle. Flatten the oval or circle and attach a variety of items with glue: a plastic gem, a ball of foil, a crumpled foil candy wrapper, a circle of cardboard covered with glitter or sequins, a star sticker, a bead, or a colorful stone.

FOIL RING: Roll up a 2" square of aluminum foil and form a circle with it. Twist the ends together to fit the finger.

TWIST TIE RING: Glue a twist tie to the center of a $\frac{1}{4}$" wide strip of construction paper or gift wrap. Decorate the paper with sequins, glitter, or foil. Wear the Ring by gently twisting it at the back of the finger.

Earrings *(DRAWING 64)*

PAPER TOWEL TUBE EARRING: Cover two 1" sections of paper towel tube with aluminum foil. Put a plastic gem, sequins, or glitter on one side of the foil-covered tube, as desired. Punch a hole in one side of the tube and thread a 5" piece of yarn through the hole. Tie the ends of the yarn together to form a loop. To wear the Paper Towel Tube Earrings, hang the loop over the ears.

BEAD EARRING: String a large bead on a 5" loop of yarn. Wear by hanging the loop over the ears.

BUTTON EARRING: Coat buttons with glitter on one side or both sides. Thread yarn through the button holes and tie the yarn in a loop to wear over the ears.

CHENILLE STEM CHAIN EARRING: Cut several 2" length chenille stems. Twist one stem together to form a ring. Place a second stem through the ring and twist it to form a two–link chain. Do the same with a third stem. Tie a loop of yarn through the top link to create a Chenille Stem Chain Earring *(SEE DRAWING 64).*

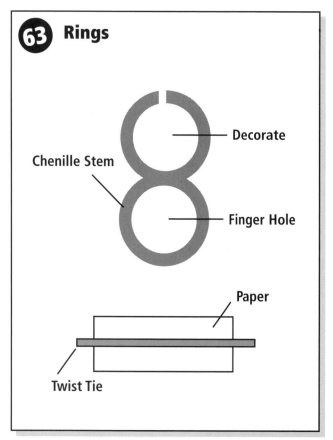

63 Rings

Chenille Stem

Decorate

Finger Hole

Paper

Twist Tie

64 Earrings

Loop

Paper Towel Tube

Loop

Bead

Loop

Button

Loop

Chenille Stem Chain

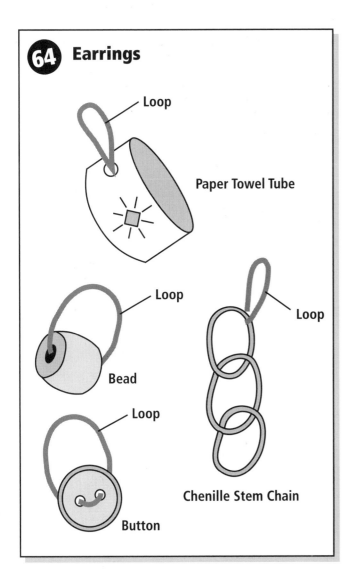

Necklaces *(DRAWING 65)*

PAPER TOWEL TUBE NECKLACE: Cut a cardboard paper towel tube into 1" sections. Cover each section with foil. Punch a hole in both sides of each section. Thread them on a 14"–18" piece of yarn. Tie shorter necklaces around the neck; slip longer necklaces over the head. Wear Paper Towel Tube Necklaces plain or decorate each foil-covered section with glitter, stickers, sequins, or plastic gems.

CUT FOIL NECKLACES: Cut a 12" × 12" piece of aluminum foil (heavy-duty works best). Fold the foil in half and place a 24" piece of yarn along the fold between the foil, leaving 6" of yarn hanging from both sides. Glue the folded foil together with a light application of glue. Allow the piece to dry, then cut the side opposite the yarn. Cut a fringe or a pattern of squares, scallops, or points. Add glitter, plastic gems, or sequins as desired. Use the yarn ties to secure the Cut Foil Necklace around the neck.

65 Necklaces

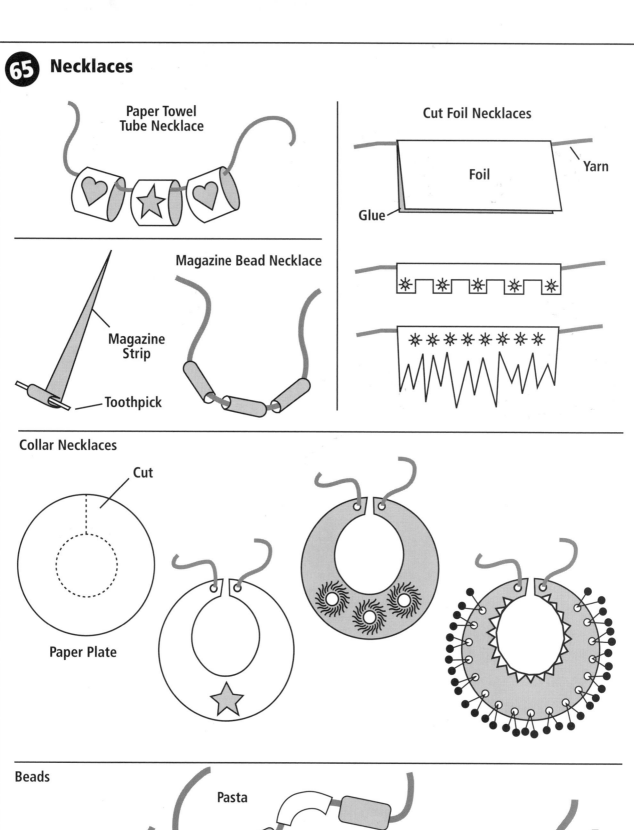

Paper Towel Tube Necklace

Magazine Bead Necklace

Magazine Strip

Toothpick

Cut Foil Necklaces

Foil

Glue

Yarn

Collar Necklaces

Cut

Paper Plate

Beads

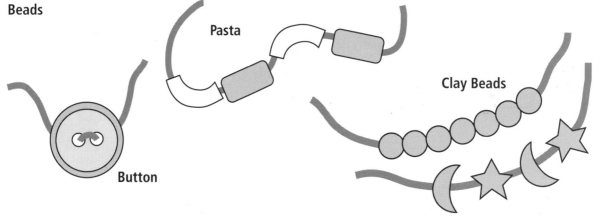

Pasta

Button

Clay Beads

COLLAR NECKLACE: Cut an 8"–10" circle from poster board or lightweight cardboard. Remove a 4"–6" oval from the circle. Cut the circle apart and taper both ends so that they are slightly narrower than the front piece. Punch a hole in both tapered ends and tie yarn through each hole (for the necklace attachment). Cover the front of the necklace completely with foil or with cut foil stars, crescents, ovals, and diamonds. Use a variety of other items to further decorate Collar Necklaces, such as plastic gems, glitter, fabric scraps, bows, pompoms, and tissue paper flowers.

For an interesting variation, make a Paper Plate Collar Necklace. Simply remove the center from a paper plate, leaving the rim. Cut the rim apart and punch a hole in each end. Tie yarn through the holes. Color or paint the necklace, or glue tissue paper scraps around the rim. Attach tissue paper flowers, plastic gems, or glitter to further embellish. Decorate all the way around the necklace or just on the front. For even fancier Collar Necklaces, punch a row of holes around the bottom edge. Space the holes at 1" or 2" intervals. Lace ribbon through the holes or hang decorative items from each hole, such as a bell, a bow, a bead, a button, or a polystyrene foam shape.

BUTTON NECKLACE: Cover large buttons with foil, glitter, or sequins. String one or several on yarn, using the excess yarn to tie the Button Necklace around the neck. Multiple buttons can be separated on the yarn by a series of knots or a 4" piece of ribbon tied in a bow.

PASTA NECKLACE: String pasta in its natural color or dye several batches (p. 143 before stringing. Use a variety of colors, shapes (so long as they have a hole for stringing), and sizes. Try painting pasta gold or silver or coating it with glue and glitter before stringing. A coat of sealer or varnish on finished beads will make them more durable and longer lasting.

MAGAZINE BEAD NECKLACE: Cut colorful, glossy magazine pages into long, narrow triangular strips with 8"–10" sides and a 1" base. Starting at the base, roll the triangle onto a toothpick or a cotton swab (with the cotton end removed). Use a dab of glue to secure the pointed end. Slide the finished bead off the toothpick or swab. Use a large needle and heavy string to thread the beads. Make a necklace with 1–3 beads in the center, or fill up an entire string with the Magazine Beads.

CLAY BEAD NECKLACE: Use a self-hardening clay (p. 140) or an oven-hardening clay (p. 141) to make beads. Roll the clay into balls or ovals. Or, roll the clay into a $\frac{1}{2}$" thick 3"–4" long roll and slice off into cylinder-shaped beads. Make a hole with a toothpick or skewer before air drying or baking. The clay can be tinted with food coloring before making the beads or the beads can be painted with acrylic paint once they harden. Hardened beads can also be painted gold or silver or brushed with glue and rolled in glitter. For a more natural look, try leaving the beads plain. A sealer will protect beads and make them last longer. String one, several, or many beads on string or thin ribbon.

SPARKLE-CLAY BEAD NECKLACE/MEDALLION: Follow the directions for this unusual clay (p. 142) and roll large 1"–2" beads. Line the beads on skewers to dry, turning them frequently to prevent sticking and to keep the holes open. String 1–4 beads on yarn or ribbon to create a Sparkle-Clay BeadNecklace/ Medallion.

Cookie cutter shapes can also be used with this clay; miniature cutters work very well. After molding, place a hole in the top of the shape and dry. String one shape or more on yarn or ribbon for a Sparkle-Clay Necklace (or Medallion).

Medallions *(DRAWING 66)*

LID MEDALLION: Paint the metal lid from a frozen juice can, or cover it with foil or gift wrap. Glue items such as plastic gems, foil star stickers, glitter, a coil of yarn, a bow, or a flower to the front of the lid for added decoration. Attach yarn to the lid in either of two ways: use masking tape to fasten the yarn to the back of the lid or use a hammer and nail to pound a hole in the lid. For the latter method, lay the lid on a block of wood and pound a nail into the top of the lid. Remove the nail and smooth any jagged edges around the hole by placing a towel on the lid and flattening the edges with a hammer. Tie yarn through the hole. Make the hole before painting or decorating Lid Medallions.

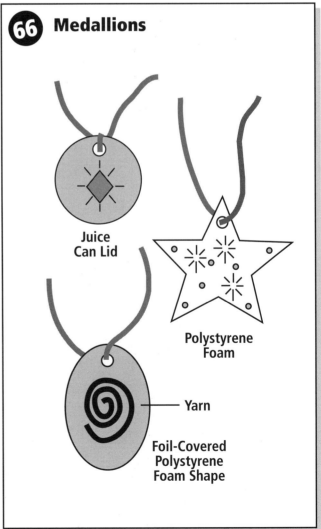

66 **Medallions**

Juice Can Lid

Polystyrene Foam

Yarn

Foil-Covered Polystyrene Foam Shape

POLYSTYRENE FOAM MEDALLION: Cut a polystyrene foam food tray into 2"–3" shapes, such as a diamond, a star, a heart, a circle, a square, a triangle, or an oval. Punch a hole in the top, for yarn, string, or ribbon. Cover the polystyrene foam shape with glitter or sequins, or attach a plastic gem to the center. Try covering the Polystyrene Foam Medallion with aluminum foil before adding glitter or gems.

A fun idea for foil-covered polystyrene foam is embossing. Cover the shape with foil; then use a blunt instrument, such as a craft stick or the end of a paintbrush, to lightly press or draw a design into the foil. Try embossing the first letter of children's names in this way. For a different embossed look, glue yarn, in the form of a border, design, or letter, onto the polystyrene foam shape; then cover the shape with foil and press it firmly against the yarn so that the piece looks like molded metal.

SHRINKIE MEDALLION/NECKLACE: Follow the directions for shrinking plastic lids and polystyrene foam (p. 145). String a variety of shrinkie shapes on one necklace or string one larger shrinkie on a medallion. Try adding glitter to Shrinkie Medallions/Necklaces by dabbing glue in the center or around the edge of the shrinkie and sprinkling glitter on the glued area.

Idea Starter

FAMILY CRESTS: Create Shields (p. 133) with children to celebrate their own families and traditions. Choose three to five symbols that represent the family: the first initial of a family name, a favorite color, a stencil of the family house or pet, a representation of a favorite family pastime (fishing, boating, etc.). Cut the symbols from felt or paper and glue them on the shield. When not being used for play, let the child hang the shield in his or her bedroom.

Bracelets *(DRAWING 67)*

Use any of the following necklace techniques to make wrist or ankle bracelets:

- Button Bracelet
- Pasta Bracelet
- Magazine Bead Bracelet
- Clay Bead Bracelet
- Sparkle-Clay Bead Bracelet

PLASTIC LID BRACELETS: Remove (cut off) the rim of the plastic lid from a margarine container, yogurt container, or peanut can. Remove a circle from the center of the lid so that a 1" ring of plastic remains. If necessary, cut through one side of the ring so that it will slip easily over the wrist. Decorate Lid Bracelets in a number of ways:

- Cover the ring with aluminum foil.
- Add plastic gems, foil stars, or glitter-covered polystyrene foam shapes to the foil-wrapped lids.

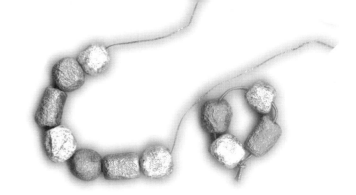

- Wrap yarn around the ring. Use one color or change colors frequently to create a multi-colored look. Secure the ends of the yarn with glue.

- Punch holes at $\frac{1}{2}$" intervals around the plastic rim. Tie yarn or ribbon through each hole to make a fringed bracelet. Try tying decorative objects to the yarn, such as bells, novelty charms, large beads, pasta, buttons, or polystyrene foam shapes.

- Brush the bracelet with glue and coat it with glitter.

- Cover the bracelet with tufts of tissue paper.

PAPIER–MÂCHÉ BANGLE: Cut a 1" x 7"–9" length of poster board or lightweight cardboard. Form the strip into a bracelet shape and staple it so that it fits over the hand. Tear newspaper into 1" x 6" strips. Dip the strips in a glue and water mixture (2 parts white glue to 1 part water).

Pull the strip through the fingers to remove excess liquid. Wrap the wet strips around the poster board ring, overlapping when necessary, until the bangle is completely covered. Let the first layer dry; repeat the procedure, adding two or three more layers. When the Papier–Mâché Bangle is completely dry, paint it with one or two base coats of white. Then decorate the bangle with acrylic paint, dimensional paint, markers, or gold and silver paint. Or, try covering the Papier–Mâché Bangle with a coat of white glue and decorating it with torn pieces

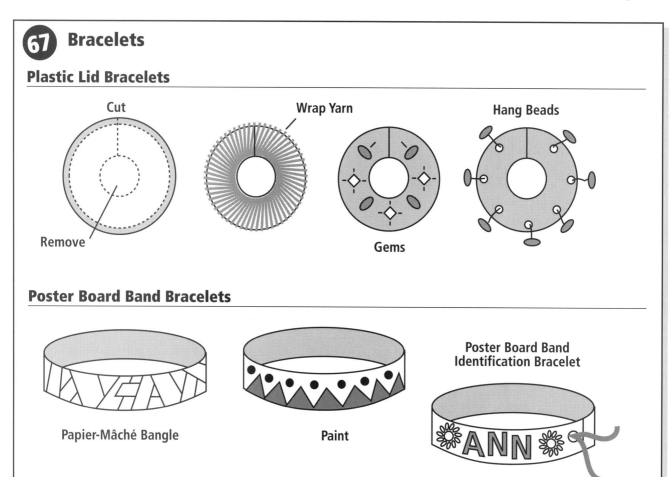

of tissue paper. Glue plastic gems, sequins, and glitter to painted or tissue-covered bangles. For added protection, apply a sealer.

PAPER TOWEL TUBE BRACELET: Cut a paper towel tube in fourths; cut apart on the diagonal (many tubes have a line to follow). Reshape the section into a bracelet shape with a larger opening ($2\frac{1}{2}$") than the original ($1\frac{1}{2}$"). Use tape to reattach the section so that it will slip comfortably over the hand. Decorate the tube section in any of the following ways: cover with foil, gift wrap, or construction pape; glue on plastic gems, sequins, or pompoms; add stickers.

POSTER BOARD BAND BRACELET: Cut a 1"–7" × 9" strip of poster board or lightweight cardboard. Decorate the strip with markers, paint, or paper scraps. Punch a hole in both ends and tie a piece of yarn through both holes (for wrist attachment). This kind of bracelet makes a fun Identification Bracelet. Write the child's name on the strip before decorating it.

Pins *(DRAWING 68)*

LID PIN: Cover the plastic lid from a frozen juice can with a circle of aluminum foil, gift wrap, construction paper, or felt. Glue plastic gems, glitter, sequins, tissue paper flowers, or felt shapes on top of covered lids. Attach a safety pin with a piece of masking tape to the back of the Lid Pin.

FELT PIN: Cut 1" shapes from felt: stars, crescents, circles, ovals, hearts, flowers, or crosses (Red Cross). Cut a second background shape out of a different color, about 1" larger. Cut a slit

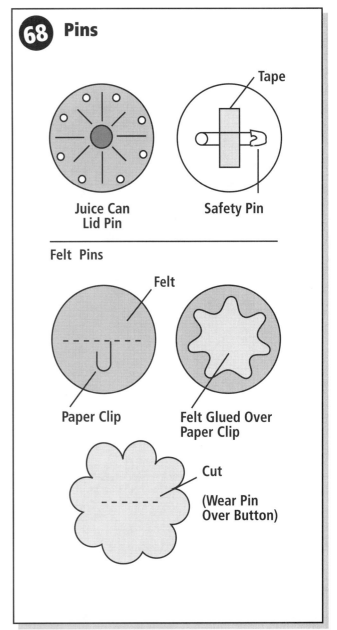

68 Pins

Tape

Juice Can Lid Pin

Safety Pin

Felt Pins

Felt

Paper Clip

Felt Glued Over Paper Clip

Cut

(Wear Pin Over Button)

in the center of the larger shape. Spread a paper clip apart and place one section of the clip in the slit. Use glue to hold the clip in place and glue the smaller felt shape on top of the larger one. (The paper clip section will rest between the two shapes.) Decorate the front of the pin with glitter, buttons, plastic gems, yarn, or ribbon. Use the paper clip section on the back to attach Felt Pins to pockets, collars, hats, and shirt necks.

Make the same type of Felt Pin using only one shape. Cut a slit in the top or center of the shape. Attach the Felt Pin to a button on the child's clothing.

Badges *(DRAWING 69)*

LID BADGE: Follow the directions for Lid Pins, p. 111. Cut the shape of a shield, circle, or star out of felt or an aluminum foil baking pan. Use dimensional paint or markers to print numbers and letters on the Lid Badges.

POLYSTYRENE FOAM BADGES: Follow the directions for Polystyrene Foam Medallions, p. 109. Emboss numbers or letters on the badges. Attach a safety pin to the back of the Polystyrene Foam Badge with a piece of masking tape.

PHOTO SLEEVE BADGE AND NAME TAGS: Use clear plastic photograph sleeves from wallets to make badges, emblems, and name tags that can be reused. Cut poster board or lightweight cardboard rectangles slightly smaller than the sleeve. Use markers, stickers, colored tape, and paper shapes to decorate the poster board.

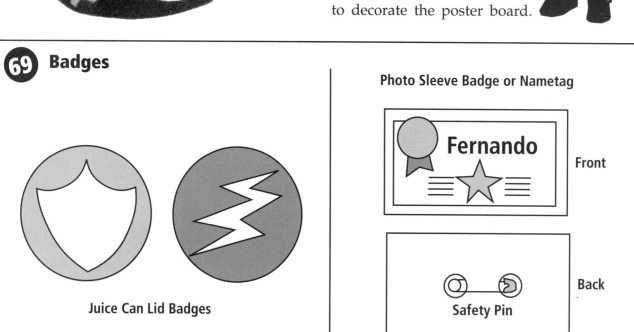

69 **Badges**

Juice Can Lid Badges

Photo Sleeve Badge or Nametag

Fernando

Front

Safety Pin

Back

Add numbers, letters, and names. Punch two holes in the back portion of the photo sleeve and place a safety pin through the holes. Slip the poster board into the sleeve and use the safety pin to attach the Photo Sleeve Badge to clothing.

Wings (DRAWING 70)

Trace a wing pattern onto poster board or lightweight cardboard. Cut out. Cut two slits or holes in the middle of each wing. Tie a 10"–14" piece of elastic cord through each set of slits (or holes). Children wear the wings by slipping the elastic over the arms and around the shoulders. Poster board is lightweight and serves as an ideal base for a variety of materials.

(SEE PATTERNS pp. 170–173.)

TISSUE PAPER WINGS: Cut the desired wing pattern from poster board. Add the slits and elastic. Tear tissue paper into large and small pieces. Use all one color or a variety of colors. Spread a light coat of white glue on the wing base. Lay the tissue paper pieces on the glue, overlapping slightly to cover the entire area. For thicker, more dimensional wings, try attaching the tissue paper in tufts or bunches.

Make Butterfly Wings by drawing an identical design on both poster board wings with a black marker. Go over the lines several times to make them thick and dark. Then fill in the areas between the lines with pieces of flat or tufted tissue paper.

BIRD WINGS: Cut two 10" × 18"-20" rectangles of felt. Make a decorative cut on one 10" side of one piece: deep scallops, long points, or wide fringe. Use glue to attach a feather to each scallop, point, or fringe piece. You can use craft feathers or make your own feathers (p. 103).

Place four holes 2" apart, on the plain end of each piece. Fold this side 4" down and mark the hole placement. Unfold and use the marks to place four additional holes in each piece. Cut four 12" pieces of yarn. Refold the felt, match the holes on each wing, and lace a piece of yarn through each set of four holes, two yarn ties per side.

To wear the bird wings, flip the felt sleeve over the arm and tie snugly. The wing fits the upper arm with feathers hanging down.

CELLOPHANE WINGS: Cut the desired wing pattern. Add the slits and elastic. Cut 4" squares of cellophane and round the corners. Squeeze the center of the squares and, stapling through this area, attach the squares to the edges of the wings. Arrange the cellophane squares so that they are close together. Staple three or four rows this way. Decorate the interior of the wings with paint or markers. Alternatively, place cellophane in the interior of the wings, for a transparent look. After assembling the poster board base, use a utility knife to cut several openings in the interior of the wings, leaving at least a 1" uncut border or edge. Cut cellophane pieces to fit the cutout sections. Tape the cellophane to the underside of the wings so that it covers the open sections. Finish the wings by stapling the rounded squares of cellophane along the edge.

TULLE (NETTING) WINGS: Cut the desired wing pattern. Add the slits and elastic. Cut four pieces of tulle netting, each 18" × 48". Lay the four pieces on top of each other and bunch the 48" width together in the center. Tie a ribbon around the center, pulling tightly to secure the tulle. Use the tip of a pair of scissors to make two holes in the center of the wing base. Thread the ends of the ribbon through the holes and tie the

Tissue Paper

Elastic

Black Plastic

Tufts of Cellophane or Tissue

Foil or Gift Wrap

Tie Tulle in Center

Tulle

Paint

Tie Bubble Wrap in Center

Bubble Wrap

Sponge Paint and Glitter

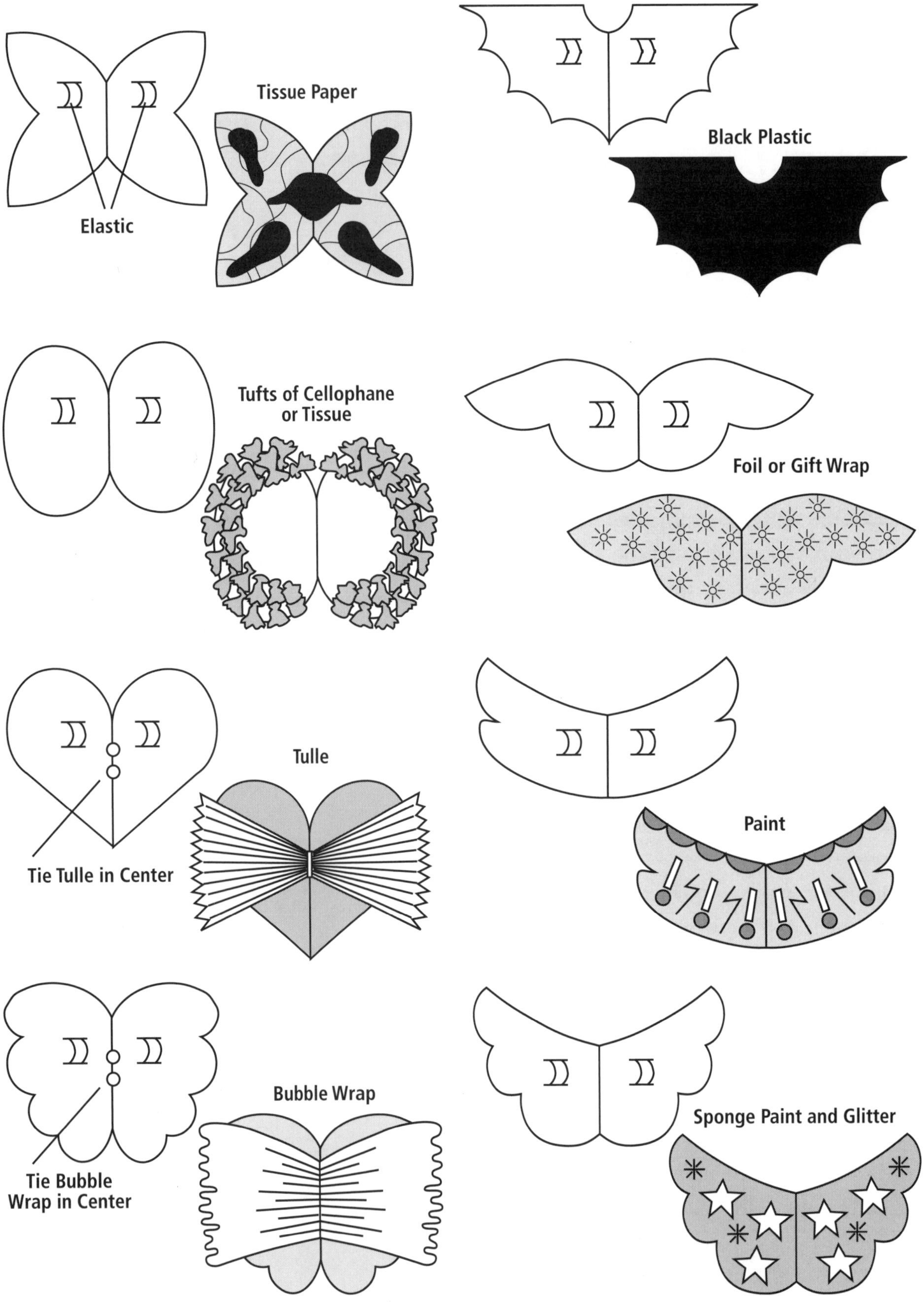

From *Nifty, Thrifty, No-Sew Costumes & Props* published by Good Year Books. Copyright © 1998 Good Year Books.

ribbon in a knot on the back, to hold the tulle on the poster board wing base. Trim the edges of the tulle to fit the shape of the wings. Further secure the tulle to the wing base with several staples along the edges. The Tulle Wings can be decorated by gluing plastic gems, sequins, bows, or glitter to the tulle.

BUBBLE WRAP WINGS: Cut the desired wing pattern. Add the slits and elastic. Cut a piece of bubble wrap that measures 16"–18" × 18"–24" (or tape smaller pieces together to make a piece of similar size). Gather the 24" width in the center and tie it securely with ribbon. To attach the Bubble Wrap Wings to the poster board wing base, follow the directions for Tulle Wings.

PLASTIC BAG WINGS: Cut the desired wing pattern. Add the slits and elastic. Using the wing base as a guide, cut the same wing design out of a large black (or other color) trash bag. Spread glue on the base and smooth the plastic bag form on top of the poster board. Glue a second (matching) plastic bag form on the back of the poster board. Cut two openings in the plastic where the elastic must come through. Plastic Bag Wings work well for insects and superhero characters.

FOIL OR GIFT WRAP WINGS: Follow the directions for the Plastic Bag Wings, except attach aluminum foil or gift wrap to a wing base.

PAINTED WINGS: Decorate a poster board wing base with paint and glitter. Acrylic and dimensional paints work especially well. Use a brush or apply the paint with a sponge. For the latter, cut one shape or a variety of shapes from a sponge. Try stars, crescents, flowers, ovals, and diamonds. Cookie cutters make great patterns for sponge shapes. Dip the damp sponge into the paint and sponge-print all over the wings. Print in a pattern, such as around the edges, to make a border, or print randomly. While the paint is still wet, sprinkle on glitter. Or, use glitter paint or metallic or glitter dimensional paint available at craft stores.

BUMBLEBEE OR BUTTERFLY WINGS: Follow the directions for Cellophane Wings, p. 113, cutting several sections inside the wings. Tape tulle (rather than cellophane) to the interior of the wings so that it covers the cutout sections.

Oxygen Tanks (DRAWING 71)

To make oxygen tanks for a diver, for example, remove the outer paper covering from two potato chip canisters. Place four holes in each can: two holes on opposite sides of the open end and two adjacent holes about $\frac{1}{2}$" apart on one side of both closed ends. Paint both cans blue, green, or gray. Run a line of glue between the cans and place several rubber bands around the joined cans until the glue dries. Holding the cans upside-down, thread a long piece of yarn through the four holes. This piece will tie around the waist. Place another piece of yarn through each pair of side holes to tie around the shoulders.

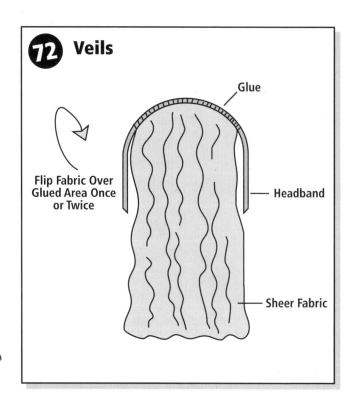

72 **Veils**

Flip Fabric Over Glued Area Once or Twice

Glue

Headband

Sheer Fabric

Veils (DRAWING 72)

Make Veils out of fabrics. Old curtains or tablecloths work well. Cut a section of sheer fabric to fit the top 4"–5" of a plastic headband. Spread glue on the top of the headband. Lay the end of the sheer fabric on the glue and press to secure. Wrap the length of fabric around the glued section once or twice more. Wear the Veil facing forward or backward, depending on how the headband is placed on the head. Make Veils as long as desired.

71 **Oxygen Tanks**

Yarn (Tie Around Arms)

Glue

Yarn (Tie Around Waist)

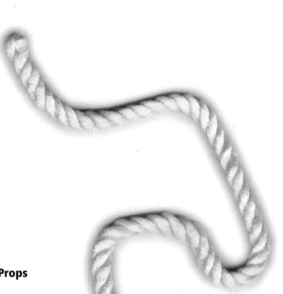

From *Nifty, Thrifty, No-Sew Costumes & Props* published by Good Year Books. Copyright © 1998 Good Year Books.

Flowers *(DRAWING 73)*

Homemade flowers accent fairy and fantasy costumes. They also have many uses with more realistic costumes, such as on hats, collars, wigs, and shoes. Attach them permanently or temporarily to a variety of dress-up clothes.

FRINGED POMPOM FLOWER: Fold a 2" × 3"–4" strip of crepe paper or felt in half to measure 1" × 3"–4". Cut into the folded edge to make a fringe. Bend the ends on the uncut side to form a circle and staple them together. Add a pompom, a circle of yarn, or a tuft of tissue paper to the center. Twist a chenille stem around the center, to form a flower stem.

FRINGED TASSEL FLOWER: Cut three to six 3" squares of tissue paper or crepe paper. Lay the squares on top of each other in a pile. Fold the pile in half. Fringe the unfolded edge. Place a chenille stem between the fold. Bend both ends of the stem down and twist them together to hold the paper in place and serve as a flower stem. Fluff out the paper fringes.

PETAL FLOWER: Wrap the end of a chenille stem around a pencil, forming a spiral. Use the spiral as the flower center and glue a pompom on the spiral. Cut six to eight petals, of any size, from crepe paper, tissue paper, or fabric. If using fabric, cut the petals with pinking shears. Place the petals around the pompom center, overlapping the petal ends on the chenille spiral. Wrap the ends onto the straight portion of the chenille stem with tape, forming the base of the flower. The remainder of the chenille forms the stem of the flower.

FLOWER BUD: Cut 3"–6" diameter circles from three colors of tissue paper, crepe paper, or fabric. If using fabric, cut with pinking shears. Lay the circles on top of each other and fold them in half. Place a chenille stem along the fold. Twist the stem together and push the paper or fabric toward the center, to form a bud. The larger the circle of paper, the larger the bud will be.

ROLLED FLOWER: Cut a 1"–2" × 8"–12" length of crepe paper or tissue paper. Roll the strip, beginning tightly in the center. Continue wrapping until the flower reaches the desired size. Hold one end while wrapping, and use a stapler or tape to secure the bottom edges when finished. Twist a chenille stem around the stapled area to serve as a flower stem.

TISSUE TUFT FLOWER: Lay four to six 3" squares or ovals of tissue paper on top of each other. Pinch the pile in the center and pick it up; twist the center and fluff out the surrounding tissue to resemble a flower. Wrap a chenille stem around the twisted center to form a flower base and stem. To make smaller or larger flowers, vary the sizes of tissue paper squares. Alternatively, make tufts of tissue paper but do not add the chenille stems. Attach to wings and other costume pieces by applying glue to the twisted center and pressing the tuft firmly on the costume.

FELT FLOWER: Cut any flower shape out of felt. Use a variety of colors and sizes. Glue green leaves to the base or back of the flowers. Layer different colors or make single-layer flowers. Cut out a small circle of felt and glue to the center, or attach a pompom. Further decorate with dimensional or fabric paint and glued-on glitter.

73 **Flowers**

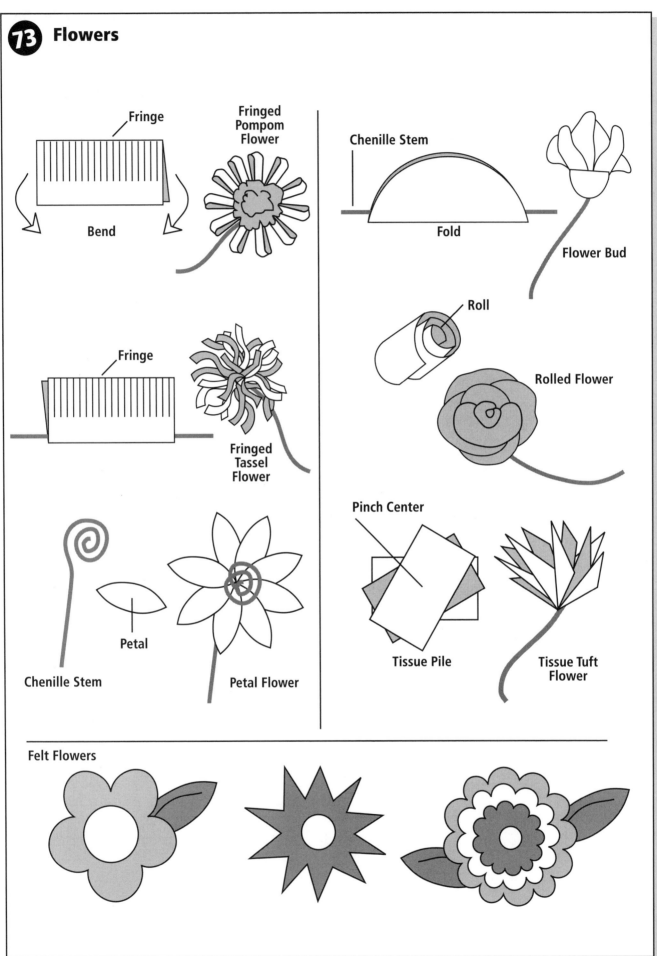

Fringe

Fringed Pompom Flower

Bend

Chenille Stem

Fold

Flower Bud

Fringe

Fringed Tassel Flower

Roll

Rolled Flower

Chenille Stem

Petal

Petal Flower

Pinch Center

Tissue Pile

Tissue Tuft Flower

Felt Flowers

Pockets

Make pockets for any tunic, vest, collar, or apron. Cut a square or rectangle of felt any size (3" × 3" and 3" × 5" work well). Cut the bottom of the pocket straight across to a point or rounded. Use Velcro to attach pockets temporarily to costumes or attach them permanently with fabric glue at the bottom and two sides. Decorate pockets with felt emblems or other decorations fastened with glue or Velcro; buttons, real or felt; or fabric or dimensional paint to mimic stitching or other decoration. Pockets on costumes can hold coins, tools, keys, a driver's license, and small notepads with pencils.

8

Props for Driving, Cooking, Fixing, and Looking: Portable Props

Children love to have something in their hands: something to turn, pull, work, point, move, and use in a variety of ways. They are also wonderful imitators who exhibit a natural curiosity about anything they see adults using. Take advantage of this by providing props and accessories that relate to a costume, but are not actually part of it. Such props offer new opportunities for creative and imaginative play. They also encourage and enhance interactions between children, offering more opportunities to verbalize, share, take turns, and negotiate.

While authentic props are certainly a wonderful choice for role play, these props are often difficult to provide—particularly in sufficient numbers. One of the most effective ways to ensure an adequate supply of a variety of props is to construct them yourself, following the guidelines provided here. *Note:* Mixing real props with handmade ones is not recommended, since real props tend to become the primary focus of the play. Additionally, handmade props require more imagination to make them become "real" to the child.

Driving Props *(DRAWING 74)*

STEERING WHEEL: Cut a 10" circle of corrugated cardboard. Draw a 9" circle inside the larger one and a letter Y within the 9" circle. Make the three sections of the letter Y 1" wide and draw the letter so that it touches the 9" circle on all three points. Use a utility knife to cut out the three sections of the circle surrounding the letter. This leaves a 1" rim around the circle and a 1" Y within the rim. Color or paint the Steering Wheel. Children hold the Steering Wheel, turning it in their hands as they move around the room.

DRIVER'S LICENSE: Use a marker to divide a 3" × 5" card in half. Glue a photograph or drawing of the child on the left side. Write the child's real or pretend name, an age, and an operator's number on the right. Cover the Driver's License with clear Contac® paper or plastic wrap.

LICENSE PLATE: Cut corrugated cardboard into a 3" × 6" rectangle. Use a black marker to write a series of six numbers and/or letters on the rectangle. Children's initials, ages, and birthdays might be used. Border the License Plate with colored tape or use a colored marker to draw a border. Punch two holes in the top and add a piece of yarn so that the License Plate can be tied on the back of a wagon, bicycle, or other vehicle.

KEYS: Trace several keys onto a polystyrene foam food tray. Cut out two of each shape and glue them together, one on top of the other. Cover the stack of two with aluminum foil. Punch a hole in the top of the finished Keys. Put several Keys on a binder ring, a key ring, a key chain, or a piece of yarn.

74 Driving Props

Cut

Cut

Steering Wheel

License Plate

Keys

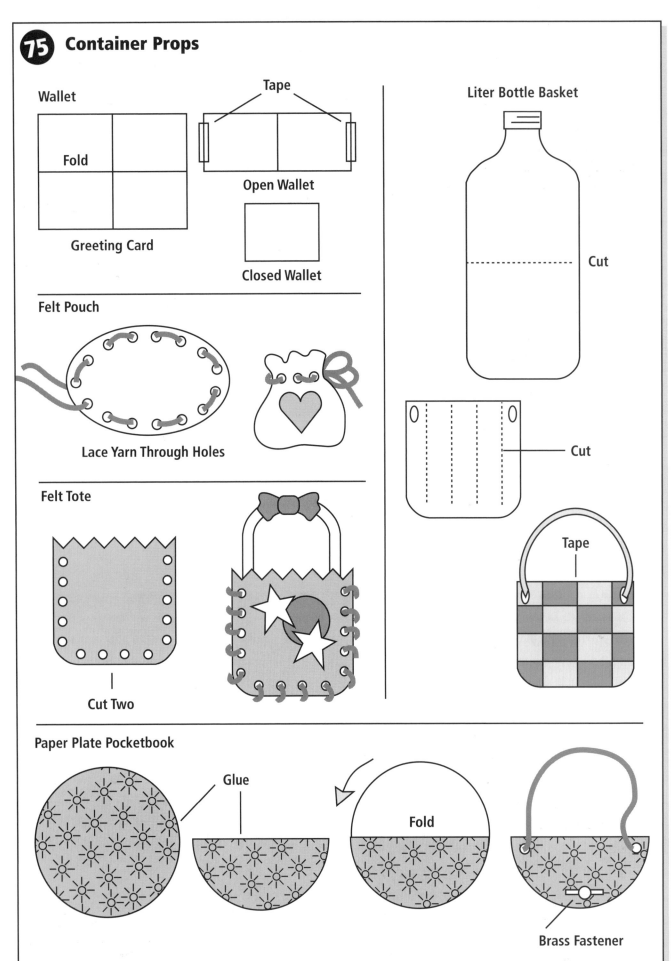

75 Container Props

Wallet

Tape

Fold

Greeting Card

Open Wallet

Closed Wallet

Liter Bottle Basket

Cut

Felt Pouch

Lace Yarn Through Holes

Cut

Felt Tote

Cut Two

Tape

Paper Plate Pocketbook

Glue

Fold

Brass Fastener

Container Props *(DRAWING 75)*

WALLET: Open out a greeting card so that it lies flat, and fold it horizontally. Fold the card in half again, this time along the original (vertical) fold. Trim the resulting Wallet to a 4" × 5" size when folded and tape the ends closed. Leave the colorful card design on the front or glue plain paper over it and decorate the Wallet with markers or crayons. Make pretend dollar bills to place in the pocket created by the horizontal fold.

FELT POUCH: Cut a felt circle or oval measuring at least 10" across. Punch holes at 1" intervals all the way around the edge, and lace a piece of yarn through the holes. Pull both ends of the yarn to gather up the felt into a Pouch. Attach bells, charms, or beads to the ends of the yarn, as desired. Children can tie the Pouch onto a belt or a sash or carry it.

FELT TOTE: Cut two pieces of felt measuring 10" × 12" each. Punch holes at 1" intervals around three sides of both felt pieces. Lay one piece of felt on top of the other. Fasten the two pieces together by lacing yarn in and out of each hole. Attach a 12"–18" piece of heavy yarn through the two top holes as a handle for the Tote. Several pieces of yarn braided together make a sturdier handle. As a variation, simply glue three edges of the two pieces of felt together. Decorate the Felt Tote with felt shapes (attach with glue), dimensional paint, or fabric paint.

NET TOTE: Start with net bags, such as those used for garlic, onions, potatoes, and oranges. Weave yarn or ribbon over and under every four to six holes. Cover the entire bag or weave several 2" stripes into the bag. Use the bag string as a handle or add a yarn handle through two of the top holes.

POCKETBOOK: Cut wallpaper, construction paper, or tissue paper into 1" × 10" strips. Tear small pieces from the strips and glue them to the back of one whole paper plate and to the back of another that has been cut in half. Tape or staple the paper plates together with the decorated backs to the outside. Fold the larger plate down over the half plate, like a flap. Place a hole in each plate where the Pocketbook will fasten. Attach a brass fastener (clasp) through the holes, from the inside of the Pocketbook to the outside. Place tape over the head of the brass fastener to keep it in place. The ends of the fastener should extend through to the front of the Pocketbook, so that children can open and close it. To make a handle for the Pocketbook, punch a hole in each side and attach yarn or ribbon.

COINS: Cut small circles of several sizes from polystyrene foam food trays or corrugated cardboard. Cover each circle with aluminum foil or glue on circles cut from shiny gift wrap or candy bar wrappers.

BASKETS: Remove the top half of a two- or three-liter plastic soda bottle and discard. Use a utility knife to cut 4" slits, spaced 1" apart, around the bottom half of the bottle. Weave yarn, ribbon, paper twist, or crepe paper over and under the slits from bottom to top. Tape the top edge, to keep the weaving in place and to cover any rough edges. Punch a hole in both sides of the Basket and attach a heavy piece of yarn to serve as a handle. A wire handle from an ice-cream container also works well. Use the same technique to make a Basket out of a large margarine or whipped topping container. For a smaller Basket, weave yarn, ribbon, paper strips, and chenille stems in and out of the openings of a plastic berry basket. Work from bottom to top. Attach a ribbon or chenille stem handle.

Looking Props *(DRAWING 76)*

BINOCULARS: Cut a cardboard paper towel tube in half. Cover both sections with construction paper or gift wrap, or decorate them with markers. Place the tubes side by side, and attach by running a line of glue between the tubes. Secure both ends with a small piece of tape. At one end, punch a hole in each side of the (attached) tube. Tie a piece of 14"–18" yarn through the holes so that the Binoculars can hang around the neck when not in use.

SPYGLASS: Decorate a paper towel tube with markers or cover it with construction paper or gift wrap. Make a second tube out of construction paper or poster board, about half the size of the first tube. Be sure to roll the paper tube slightly smaller than the cardboard tube so that it will fit inside. Place the tubes together such that the smaller paper tube can be pulled out or pushed in as the Spyglass is used.

Idea Starter

WOODWORKING FUN: Collect wood scraps, craft sticks, wooden craft shapes, sandpaper, nuts and bolts, and white glue. Make these available to children, along with some handmade related props: Power Beam (p. 126), Tools (p. 130), Tool Belt (p. 130), Tool Box (p. 130), and Construction Cone (p. 130). Children will love using real woodworking materials and these props while wearing the Construction Worker costume (p. 178).

From *Nifty, Thrifty, No-Sew Costumes & Props* published by Good Year Books. Copyright © 1998 Good Year Books.

EYEGLASSES AND SUNGLASSES: Cut two adjoining rings from a plastic six-pack holder. Trace the two rings onto construction paper, felt, or gift wrap and cut out. Glue the paper or felt rings onto the plastic rings. Twist a chenille stem around both sides of the covered rings. Bend the end of the stems to fit around the ears. (The stems can be straightened and bent again to adjust to any child's head.) Tape a circle of clear cellophane or plastic wrap over the eye holes or leave open. Make Sunglasses in the same way, except attach a circle of colored cellophane over the eye holes.

DIVER MASK: Cut a 6" × 8" polystyrene food tray in half. Remove a 2" × 4" rectangle from the center of the tray. Cut a notch in the lower center to fit over the nose. Tape a piece of clear plastic or cellophane on the back of the tray over the opening, or leave open. Punch a hole in both sides and add yarn so that the Diver Mask can be tied behind the head. The polystyrene foam part of the mask can be covered fully or partially with felt.

76 Looking Props

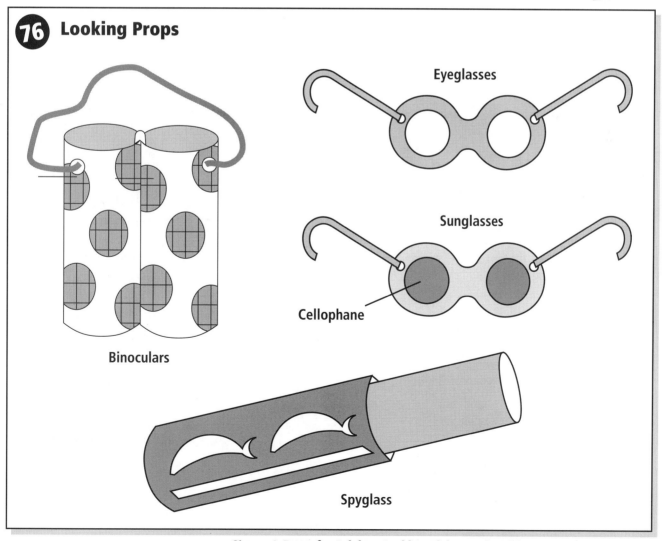

Eyeglasses

Sunglasses

Cellophane

Binoculars

Spyglass

POWER BEAM: Remove the bottom of a one-gallon, plastic water or juice jug. Brush on an acrylic paint and a sealer. The sealer will prevent the paint from being chipped off during play. Add stripes or other decorations as desired. Cover the open bottom with colored cellophane, foil or clear paper twist. Cut the cellophane slightly larger than the opening and tape it to the inside of the jug. Children can hold the handle of the jug and use the "beam" bottom as a pretend light source.

FLASHLIGHT: Cut a paper towel tube to a length of four inches. Cut a circle of cellophane (clear or colored) slightly larger than the tube opening and tape it over the end. Cover the tube with plain paper or gift wrap. Attach two brass fasteners or glue two small buttons on one side of the covered tube as "off" and "on" switches.

Cooking Props *(DRAWING 77)*

BAKING PANS: Cover polystyrene foam food trays, shoe box lids, or cereal boxes (with the fronts removed) with aluminum foil for use as Baking Pans of various sizes. Make muffin pans by removing the lids from egg cartons and covering the egg cup sections with foil. For a pizza pan, cut a 10"–12" circle of cardboard and cover it with foil. Items can also be painted with silver paint rather than covered with foil.

COOKBOOKS AND MENUS: Cut recipes from magazines or packages of food. Tape or glue them to 9" × 12" paper. Make a cover by gluing pictures of food or cooking utensils to a piece of construction paper and printing the word COOKBOOK across the top. Punch several holes along the left side of the pages and secure with yarn or brass fasteners. For menus, use pictures of food and the printed names of the food on the inside pages and the name of the restaurant on the cover page.

KITCHEN APRON: Cut a 12"–14" square of felt. Follow the procedure for the Tool Apron, p. 130, to attach one pocket and yarn or ribbon that can tie around the waist. Round the two bottom corners or make a decorative cut on the edge.

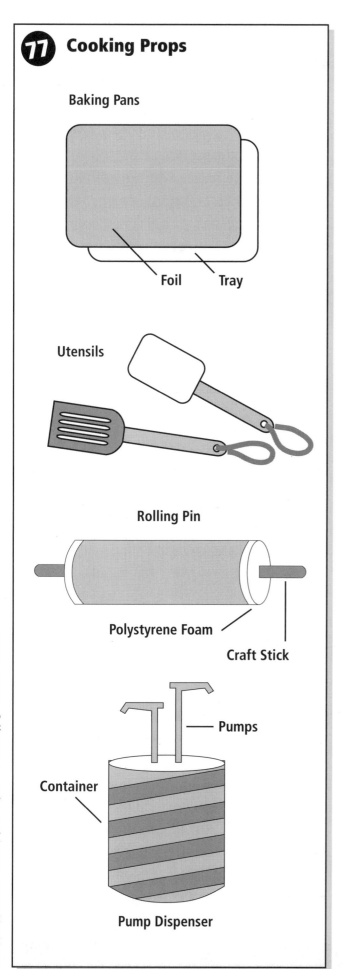

77 **Cooking Props**

Baking Pans

Foil   Tray

Utensils

Rolling Pin

Polystyrene Foam

Craft Stick

Pumps

Container

Pump Dispenser

KITCHEN UTENSILS: Trace around real kitchen utensils to make these props. Trace the smaller utensils onto large plastic coffee can lids; trace the larger utensils onto corrugated cardboard. Cut out the plastic and cardboard utensils. Color the utensils with markers or acrylic paint. If desired, punch a hole in one end of the utensil and loop a piece of yarn through it, for hanging up utensils when not in use. Trace utensils such as these:

- bread knife
- carving knife: cut one edge with pinking shears
- cutting board
- flipper
- grapefruit spoon: cut the spoon edges with pinking shears
- large fork
- measuring spoons: attach four sizes together with a brass fastener
- mixing spoon
- paring knife
- pastry brush: attach fringed paper or yarn pieces for the bristles
- pastry scraper
- pie server
- pizza cutter
- spatula

From *Nifty, Thrifty, No-Sew Costumes & Props* published by Good Year Books. Copyright © 1998 Good Year Books.

ROLLING PIN: Cut two circles of polystyrene foam, 1"–2" thick, that will fit snugly in the ends of a paper towel tube. Press a craft stick into the center of each circle. Remove the stick and coat one end of each with glue. Replace the sticks in the polystyrene foam. While the sticks are drying, cover the paper towel tube with construction paper. Tape the edges. Spread glue on the rim of the polystyrene foam circles and push one into each end of the tube. The craft sticks serve as the handles for the Rolling Pin.

PUMP DISPENSER: Use the tip of a pair of scissors to poke two or three holes in the lid of a round oatmeal container. Place several (cleaned) pumps from discarded shampoo, hand lotion, liquid soap, or syrup bottles in each hole. If necessary, cut the pump ends to the same length and cut the container shorter so that the pumps reach the bottom. Tape the lid closed and cover the Pump Dispenser with gift wrap.

Cheering Props *(DRAWING 78)*

MEGAPHONE: Remove the bottom of a one-gallon plastic water or milk jug and discard. Decorate the remainder of the jug with colored tape or dimensional paint; before painting, rough up the surface of the jug with sandpaper to help the paint adhere. After decorating and/or painting, cover rough edges with tape.

CHEERLEADING POMPOMS: Cut thirty 1" × 24" strips of tissue paper or crepe paper. Use yarn to tie the paper strips securely in the center, making a bundle of 1" × 12" strips. Place a loop of yarn through the yarn holding the strips together, so the Pompom can be held in the hand. Or, staple the Pompom to a decorated paper towel tube, so that children can hold onto something larger.

MICROPHONE: Cut a cardboard paper towel tube in half. Cover the tube with construction paper, gift wrap, or felt. Crumple a piece of aluminum foil. Attach the foil ball by placing glue around the rim of the tube and pressing the ball onto the glue. Punch a hole in the bottom of the tube and attach an 8" piece of yarn in the hole, to serve as a Microphone cord.

FLAGS AND PENNANTS: Cut an 8" × 12" felt rectangle. Glue two chenille stems on each 12" side and one stem on each 8" side. Glue the stems about 1" from the edge. Choose a color that contrasts with the felt. The chenille stems serve two purposes: they provide a decorative border and a means of support that keeps the flag straight when attached to a stick. Decorate the flag with felt shapes, pompoms, colored tape, yarn, or feathers; use glue to attach these. Tape the Flag onto a 12" dowel rod, a ruler, a wrapping paper tube, or a sturdy tree branch. To make a Pennant, follow the same procedure, except cut a 12" long triangle with a 6" base.

Prepare Felt Flags and Pennants for children to design. Make the base of the flags/pennants, using a variety of felt colors and chenille stem borders. Provide a box of precut felt shapes, pompoms, bows, and feathers. Attach self-stick Velcro dots to both the flag/pennant and the decorations, so that children can design the flags/pennants in any way they choose. After play, the flags/pennants can be taken apart and the Velcro removed, leaving the materials ready for use during the next pretend play session. Of course, child designs can always be attached permanently with glue.

78 Cheering Props

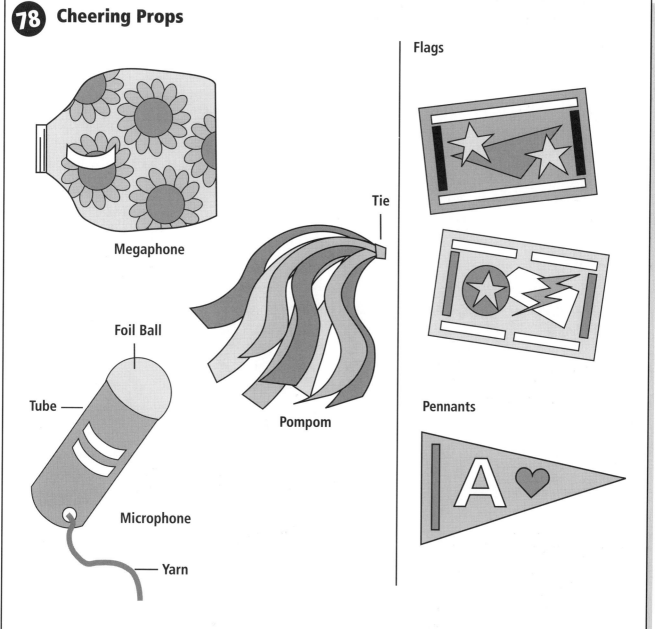

Fixing Props (DRAWING 79)

TOOLS AND TOOL BOX: Trace tools onto corrugated cardboard. Color tools with markers or acrylic paint. Wrap masking tape or colored tape around the handle section. Cover a large shoe box with construction paper or colored Contac® paper for use as a Tool Box. Trace tools such as these:

- hammer
- mallet
- saw: use pinking shears to cut the blade
- screwdriver
- wrench
- gardening tools

TOOL APRON: Cut a 15" × 5" piece of felt. Then, out of a different color of felt, cut one 3" × 4" and two 2" × 4" pieces. Attach them to the 15" × 5" piece with a stapler: attach the two smaller pieces on the outside and the larger piece in the middle, like pockets. Fabric glue can also be used for attachment. Punch holes on the top of the 12" × 5" piece at 2" intervals. Lace yarn through the holes so that the Tool Apron can be tied in the back.

Idea Starter

KITCHEN HELPER FUN: When children help in the kitchen at home or school, add Restaurant Worker costumes (p. 189) and props to the action: Menus and Cookbooks (p. 126), Kitchen Utensils (p. 127), Baking Pans (p. 126), and a Pump Dispenser (p. 128). Wearing these costume pieces and using handmade props make children's participation in kitchen activities more meaningful and fun.

TOOL BELT: Tie four to six pieces of elastic around a child's belt, in loops. Attach Cardboard Tools to it.

CHAIN: Use scraps of playground swing chains or bicycle chains or make a chain with plastic fasteners used to close trash and lawn bags. Use the fasteners that have a hole and a series of teeth that lock into the hole. Make a starter loop with one fastener and attach additional fasteners one after the other like the links of a Chain.

HOSE: Cut an old garden hose into 2' and 3' pieces. Wrap one end with silver or black tape to represent the nozzle. Or make hoses with large, black plastic trash bags. Cut a 2' length from top to bottom along both sides of the bag, leaving the side and bottom seams intact. Run a piece of clear tape along the open side. Stuff the bag tube with crumpled newspaper or plastic grocery bags. Use a yardstick to push stuffing material to the bottom. Tie the top closed and wrap silver or red tape around the tied end as a nozzle.

CONSTRUCTION CONE: Cut a 20" × 26" diameter half circle from orange poster board and form it into a cone. Fasten with tape or staples. Cut the point off the top, the excess from the inside, and trim the bottom of the cone so that it sits level.

79 **Fixing Props**

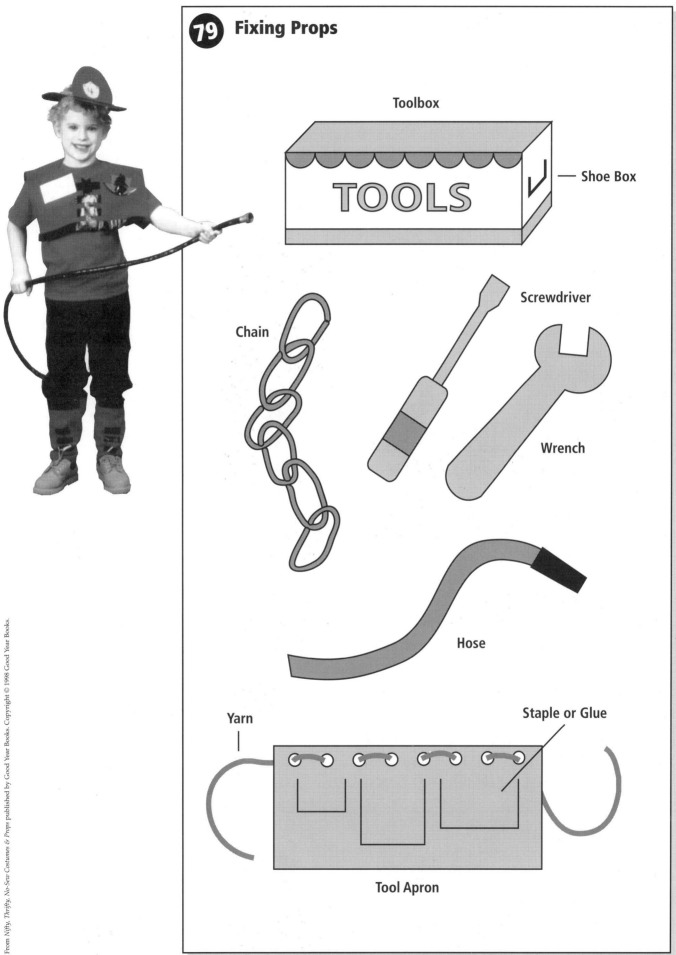

Toolbox

Shoe Box

TOOLS

Chain

Screwdriver

Wrench

Hose

Yarn

Staple or Glue

Tool Apron

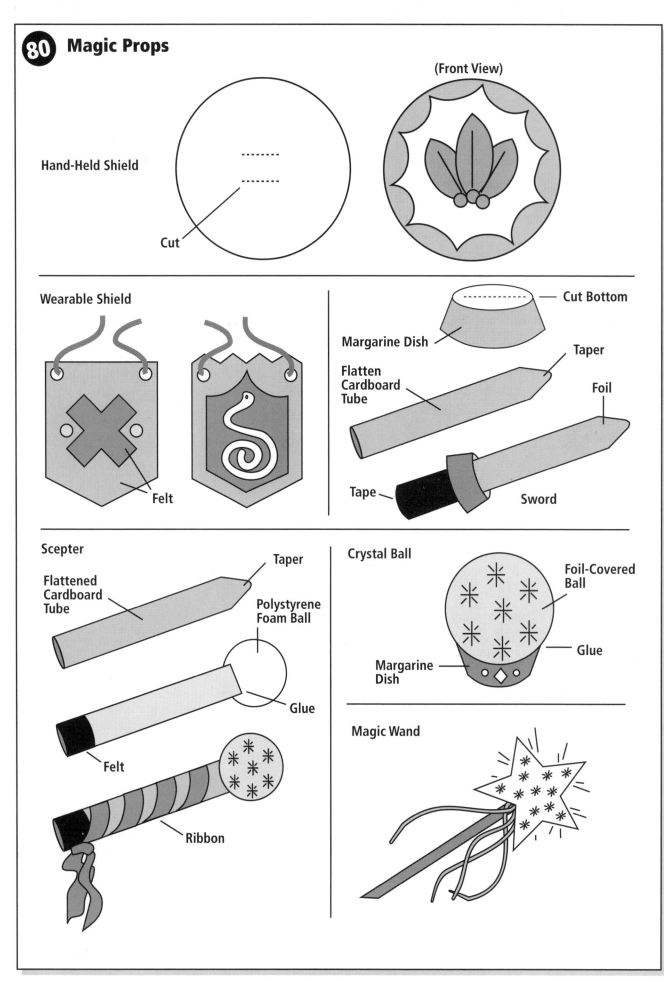

Hand-Held Shield

Cut

(Front View)

Wearable Shield

Felt

Margarine Dish — Cut Bottom

Flatten Cardboard Tube

Taper

Foil

Tape

Sword

Scepter

Flattened Cardboard Tube

Taper

Polystyrene Foam Ball

Glue

Felt

Ribbon

Crystal Ball

Foil-Covered Ball

Glue

Margarine Dish

Magic Wand

Magic Props (DRAWING 80)

SHIELDS TO HOLD: Cut a 10"–12" diameter circle of cardboard. Decorate it with markers, acrylic paints, foil, felt, or paper scraps. Cut two slits on either side of the center and tie a piece of yarn or elastic through the slits. Children hold the Shield by gripping the yarn or elastic.

To make Shields that look like metal, construct the cardboard base, then glue yarn on the circle in any pattern: a border and center design, a coat of arms, a variety of shapes or letters. Cover the entire Shield with aluminum foil, pressing the foil firmly against the yarn designs to suggest molded metal. The lid (with a handle) of a large trash can also makes a great base for a shield. Wash the lid thoroughly first. Cut a circle from heavy paper or poster board that matches the size of the lid. Decorate the circle with markers, crayons, or paint. Attach the circle inside the lid with rolled pieces of masking tape. Children can hold the handle on the lid to use the Shield.

SHIELDS TO WEAR: Cut a 9" × 12" or 9" × 14" piece of felt. Cut the 9" bottom into a point. Use contrasting colors of felt or fabric and metallic paint to decorate. Try making a coat of arms, a flash of lightning, or a star (the latter two are particularly well suited to a superhero costume). Punch two holes in the top 9" side and add yarn so that the Shield or Breastplate can be tied loosely around the neck. A second tie can be added that will fasten around the child's waist by punching a hole in each bottom corner and adding yarn. Wear alone or over a tunic.

SWORD: Make a slit in the bottom of a plastic margarine or yogurt container, then set aside. Flatten a cardboard gift wrap tube and cut the tube 22" long. Taper one end with scissors to look like the blade of a sword. Cover the flattened tube with aluminum foil. Paint the margarine container or cover it with foil (nonshiny side out). Push the untapered end of the tube through the slit in the plastic container; push through until about 4" extends out of the container. This shorter section forms the handle of the Sword. Wrap felt or plastic tape around 2" of the end.

SCEPTER: Cut a gift wrap tube in half and flatten it. Cut the tube 16" long. Use scissors to taper one end of the tube to a point. Paint the flattened tube, or cover it with foil or gift wrap. Cut a 1" × 12" strip of black or purple felt. Glue it on one end of the tube by wrapping it around about 2" of the tube. This forms the handle of the Scepter. Cover a 3"–4" polystyrene foam ball with foil. Use a pencil to poke a hole in the ball. Place glue in the hole and push the tapered end of the tube into the ball. Let the Scepter dry. Glue several plastic gems, sequins, or dots of glitter on the foil-covered ball. If desired, wind a ribbon or length of crepe paper diagonally around the tube, from the ball to the handle. Tie the ribbon at the handle end, letting the ends hang loose. Try adding several additional lengths of ribbon for a fancier Scepter.

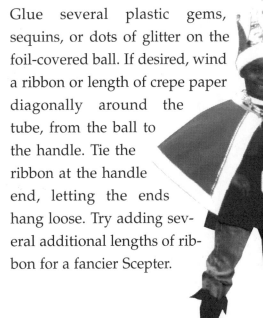

CRYSTAL BALL: Cover the sides of a margarine dish or yogurt container with gift wrap, crepe paper, or construction paper. If using construction paper, glue on glitter, plastic gems, or shapes cut from foil, such as stars, crescents, and diamonds. Cover a 4"–6" polystyrene foam ball with aluminum foil. Depending on the size of the dish or container, the size of the polystyrene foam ball may need to be adjusted. Decorate the foil ball with glitter and randomly spaced foil star stickers. Spread glue around the rim of the dish or container. Set the covered ball on the container and let dry.

MAGIC WAND: Cut a paper towel tube apart diagonally so that it forms a spiral. Some tubes have a visible line that can be followed. Reform the tube, rolling it tightly to make a thinner, sturdier rod. Cut one end, so that the rod measures 10"–12" long. Wrap the rod with aluminum foil or shiny gift wrap. Tape the edge of the paper and tuck the excess into the ends of the rod. Trace a star (a cookie cutter works well as a pattern) and cut it out. Paint the star silver or gold or brush it with glue and add glitter. Cut two notches on the bottom of the star and apply glue to the notches. Press the notched and glued end onto the wrapped rod and let dry. The star can also be taped or stapled to the rod. Tie several lengths of ribbon on the rod under the star. Let the ribbons hang straight or lightly starch and curl them around a pencil.

WIZARD WAND: Cut a paper towel tube on the diagonal, creating one long spiral. Roll the tube into a tighter, thinner tube and cut it to a length of 12". Cover the tube with felt attached with glue. Coat about two inches of one end with glue. Dip the glued end into glitter, coating it thoroughly.

Miscellaneous Props

ROPE: Cut an 8" piece and two to three yard lengths (36" each) of jute, heavy yarn, or clothesline. Wind the length of rope loosely, making loops that are about a foot long. Tie the loops together by wrapping the 8" piece around one section and securing the piece with a knot. The tied section is the top, the part that the child holds.

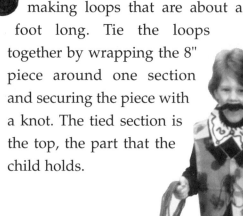

CHAPTER

9

Money-Saving Recipes

The following "recipes," for making face paint, clay beads, and so on, may be helpful and certainly will save money. Remember to be aware of any allergies before applying anything to children's skin.

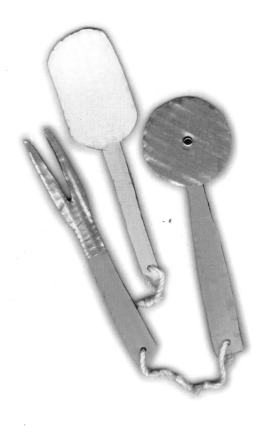

Fantastic Face Paint: A Nontoxic Homemade Makeup

· ·

Fantastic Face Paint is safe and will not harm skin.

- Combine shortening and cornstarch.

- Mix well, until the mixture resembles toothpaste.

- Add a sprinkle of flour to thicken, if necessary.

- Divide the mixture into thirds or fourths. Add several drops of food coloring to each portion, to make different colors of make-up.

Ingredients

- ■ **4 tablespoons white shortening**
- ■ **8 tablespoons cornstarch**
- ■ **sprinkle of flour, as needed**
- ■ **food coloring**
- ■ **baby powder or talcum powder**

Double or triple the recipe for larger amounts.

Apply Fantastic Face Paint with the fingertips, using cotton swabs to make fine details. As a finishing touch and to help the face paint last longer, pat decorated faces with cotton balls dusted lightly with baby powder or talcum powder. Be careful not to make a cloud of power—inhaling powder can be dangerous.

Remove with baby oil, cold cream, or petroleum jelly.

Skin Glue and Skin Designs

....

Make a skin glue that is natural and nontoxic. Use the glue to adhere 1" – 2" tissue paper shapes to cheeks, foreheads, chins, hands, or arms.

- Cook potatoes with the skins on until they are fork tender.

- Allow to cool.

- Slice the potatoes in half.

- Use the surface of the cooked potato as a glue. Cut shapes and designs from the 1"–2" tissue paper squares. Place a precut tissue paper design on the potato surface so that it absorbs the natural starch from the potato. Place the design on clean, dry skin. Use the same potato for a number of designs. Try cutting hearts, stars, suns, crescents, diamonds, flowers, birds, animals, and letters or numbers.

To remove the Skin Designs, peel them off and wash the skin with soap and water.

Skin Glue Printers

Follow the directions on the previous page for Skin Glue.

After the potato cools, make it into a printer by cutting a raised shape into the surface of the potato. Do this by removing the edges of the potato and shaping the center portion into the desired shape. Place the potato printer onto the skin and press firmly. Sprinkle glitter or confetti directly on the glue left on the skin from the potato.

To remove, wash the glitter or confetti from the skin with soap and water.

Ingredients
■ potatoes: $\frac{1}{2}$ per child
■ glitter or confetti

Homemade Dimensional or Puffy Paint

....

Make a shiny dimensional paint that can be used to trim and decorate paper, poster board, and cardboard. Put this paint in plastic squeeze bottles, such as glue, catsup, or honey bottles.

- Combine equal parts salt, flour, and water.

- Add a few drops each of white glue and food coloring. Mix well.

Use a funnel to transfer the paint into the squeeze bottles. Mix several different colors.

Ingredients

- salt
- flour
- water
- white glue
- food coloring

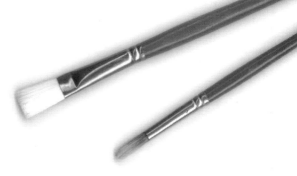

Bead Clay: Self-Hardening

Beads made with this clay will dry overnight. In addition to round or oval beads, try other shapes, such as cylinders, hearts, flat disks, triangles, diamonds, and crescents

Ingredients

- $1\frac{1}{2}$ cups flour
- 1 cup salt
- 1 cup cornstarch
- warm water

- Mix flour, salt, and cornstarch.

- Slowly add warm water until the mixture holds its shape.

- Knead the clay for several minutes before rolling and forming beads.

- Pierce each bead with a toothpick before drying; let dry overnight.

To decorate paint with acrylic or tempera paint (colors or gold and silver). Add shapes, lines, and dots with dimensional paint. Dot with glue and add glitter or cover with glue and roll in glitter.

To make colored clay that needs no painting, add food coloring to the water before mixing.

Bead Clay: Oven-Hardening

•••••••••••••••••••••••••••

Make this clay just before using it, and bake finished pieces immediately. Beads should not be too large, or the clay will not bake in the center. Store unused clay in a covered container.

Ingredients

- **4 cups flour**
- **1 cup salt**
- **$1\frac{1}{2}$ cups warm water**

- Combine salt and flour.

- Gradually add warm water, stirring until the mixture is well blended.

- Turn the clay onto a floured surface and knead 4–5 minutes.

- Roll small beads and pierce each with a toothpick. Flat shapes such as ovals, circles, hearts, triangles, and diamonds work well. Cut shapes with a knife or use small cookie cutters. Poke a hole in the top of flat shapes before baking.

- Place beads on a baking sheet. Bake beads in a 300°F oven until hard, approximately 30 minutes, but this varies depending on thickness of clay. Note: This is an adult project, since it requires a hot oven. Children can help with the cutting and decorating.

To decorate follow the same suggestions for self-hardening clay, p. 140.

Sparkle Clay

• •

This is a self-hardening clay, which dries overnight. The rock salt adds a crystal sparkle to the finished bead.

- Combine white glue and liquid starch.

- Add several drops of food coloring to the mixture.

- Stir in rock salt.

Ingredients
■ $\frac{1}{4}$ cup white glue
■ $\frac{1}{4}$ cup liquid starch
■ food coloring
■ 1 cup rock salt

To decorate dab on glue and add glitter or attach sequins or plastic gems with glue. Since this clay is colored and contains the sparkle of rock salt, little decoration is needed.

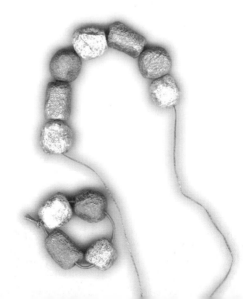

Dyed Pasta

Dye pasta for jewelry making.

- Place pasta in a large glass jar or plastic freezer bag.

- Put several drops of food coloring in 1–3 teaspoons of water, depending on the intensity of the color desired.

- Add the liquid to the pasta and shake vigorously.

- Spread the dyed pasta on wax paper to dry. Turn the pieces several times during drying.

Ingredients

- 1 cup dry pasta
- food coloring
- 1-3 teaspoons water

Papier-Mâché Glue

· ·

Saturate newspaper strips in glue-and-water mixture to create Papier-Mâché items that, when dry, are quite hard and durable.

Ingredients

- ■ **2 cups white glue**
- ■ **1 cup water**

- Combine white glue and water.

- Stir the mixture until it is well blended.

- Dip newspaper strips into the mixture and then slide them through the fingers to remove excess liquid.

- Place the strips over your base, overlapping the strips to cover completely.

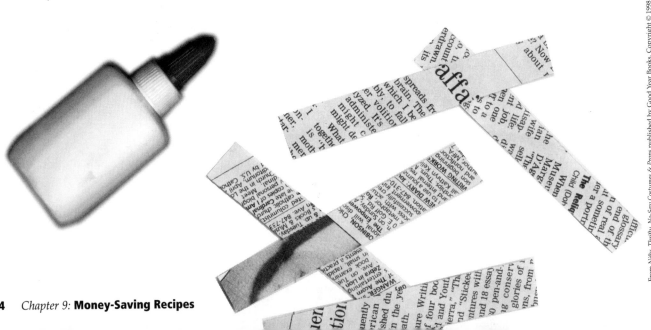

Plastic and Polystyrene Foam Shrinkies

. . . .

Recycle plastic lids from coffee cans, polystyrene foam food trays, and egg cartons into necklace or bracelet charms in minutes. *Note:* This is an adult project, since it requires a hot oven. Children can help with the cutting and decorating.

Ingredients

- clear plastic lids
- polystyrene foam food trays and egg cartons
- permanent markers
- yarn

- Cut plastic lids and polystyrene foam into a variety of shapes; shapes should be no smaller than 3" × 4".

- Decorate the shapes with permanent markers.

- Poke a hole in the top of each shape.

- In a well-ventilated area, bake the shapes in a 350°F oven for 3–4 minutes.

- If the edges of the shapes curl up, flatten them with a spatula while the shapes are still warm.

- Thread yarn through the holes to create a necklace or bracelet.

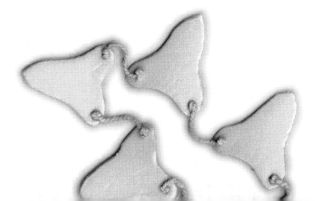

CHAPTER 10

Reproducible Patterns

Several of the reproducible patterns in this section are drawn to scale. Simply trace the pattern onto cardboard or posterboard to make sturdy, reusable patterns. Construction paper, newspaper, and grocery bag paper make good temporary or one-use patterns.

Most of the patterns are based on a scale of 1" = 3", 1" = 4", or 1" = 5", as designated. So, for example

A 1" = 4" scale
With a pattern that measures $3\frac{1}{2}$" $\times$ 9"
Converts to a finished size of 14" $\times$ 36"

These reduced size patterns illustrate proportion. Use the full-size dimensions given on the pattern to draw a full-size pattern onto construction paper, newspaper, or grocery bag paper.

Before using your pattern, try it on the child or children you are making costumes for to check the dimensions. Make any adjustments in size that are necessary to give the look, length, and width you desire. Finally, use the paper pattern or transfer your final pattern onto cardboard or posterboard for a more sturdy, reusable pattern. Measure your final pattern to determine the amount of felt or other material to buy.

Remember to put scraps to use making accessories and props!

Basic Tunic Pattern

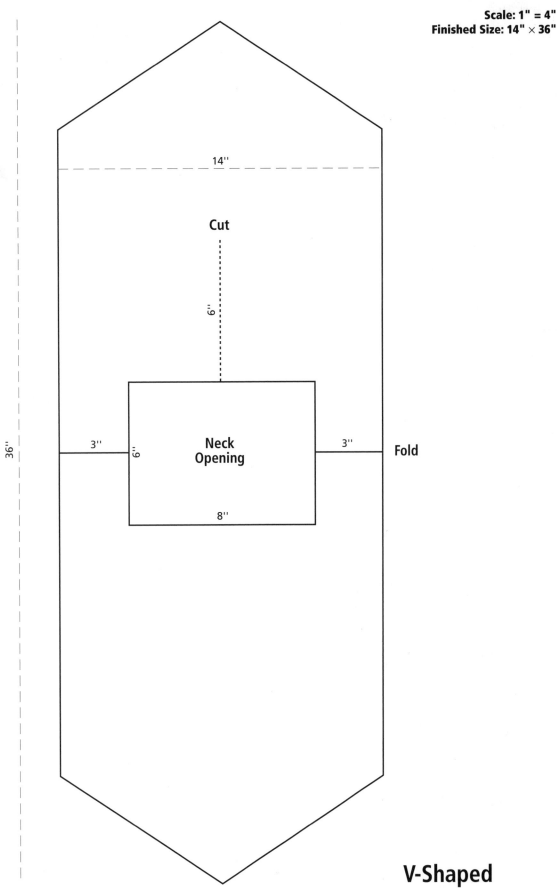

14''

Cut

6''

Neck
Opening

3''   6''   3''   Fold

8''

36''

V-Shaped

Pattern is shown in reduced size but labeled with full-size dimensions.

Basic Tunic Pattern

Scale: 1" = 4"
Finished Size: 14" × 36"

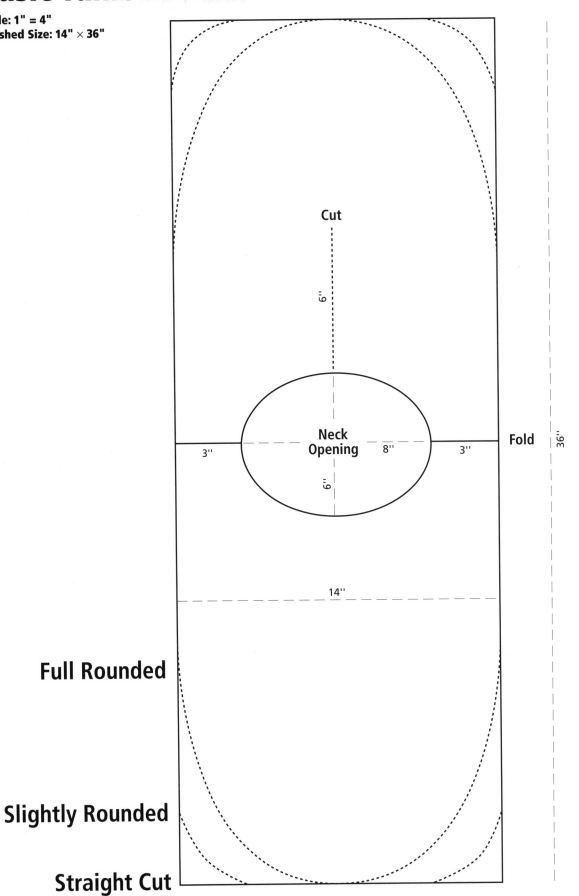

Cut

6"

Neck
Opening

3"   8"   3"   Fold

6"

36"

14"

Full Rounded

Slightly Rounded

Straight Cut

Pattern is shown in reduced size but labeled with full-size dimensions.

Basic Tunic Pattern

Scale: 1" = 4"
Finished Size: 14" × 36"

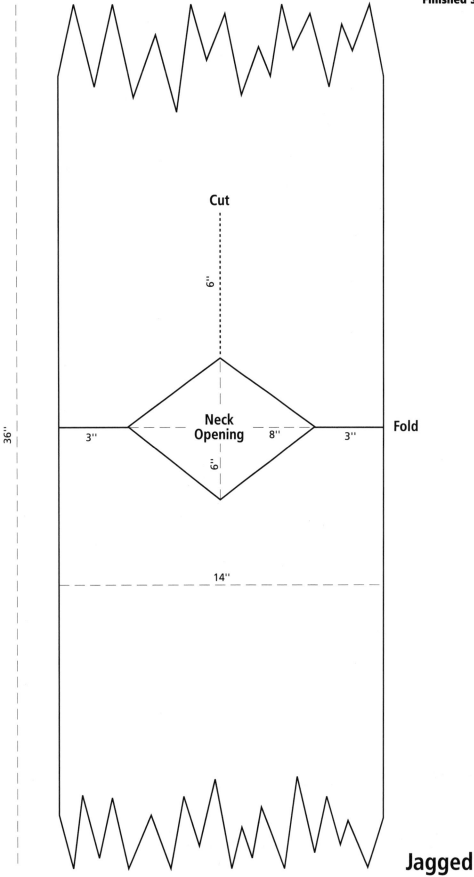

Cut

6''

Neck
Opening

3''   8''   3''   Fold

36''

14''

Jagged

Pattern is shown in reduced size but labeled with full-size dimensions.

Basic Tunic Pattern

Scale: 1" = 4"
Finished Size: 14" × 36"

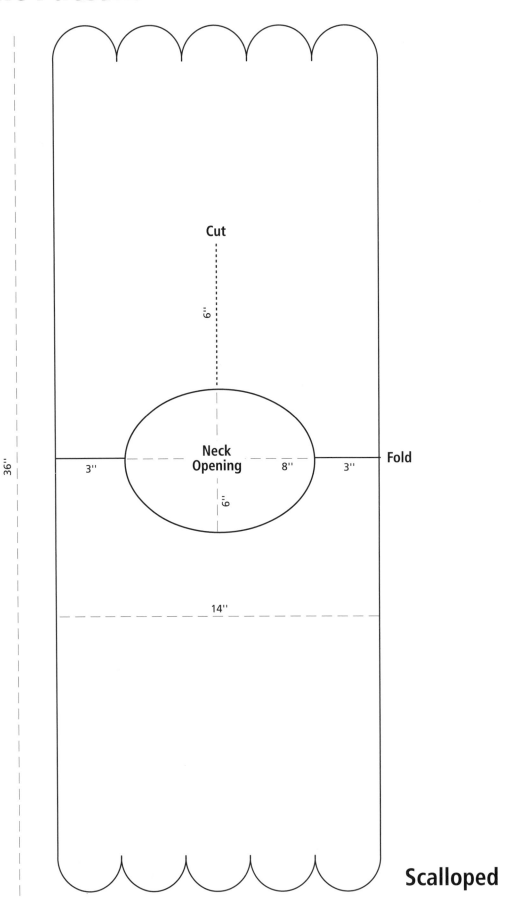

Cut

6"

36"

Neck
Opening

3"   8"   3"

Fold

6"

14"

Scalloped

Pattern is shown in reduced size but labeled with full-size dimensions.

Basic Tunic Pattern

Scale: 1" = 4"
Finished Size: 14" × 36"

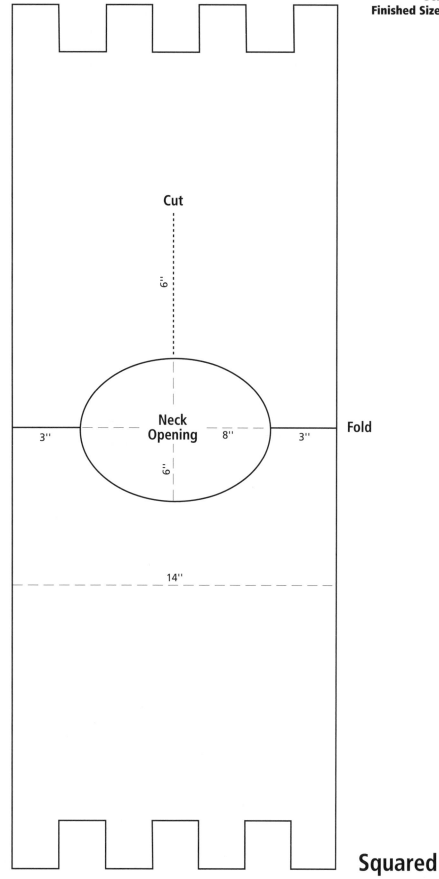

Cut

6"

Neck
Opening

3"   8"   3"   Fold

36"

6"

14"

Squared

Pattern is shown in reduced size but labeled with full-size dimensions.

Basic Tunic Pattern

Scale: 1" = 4"
Finished Size: 14" × 36"

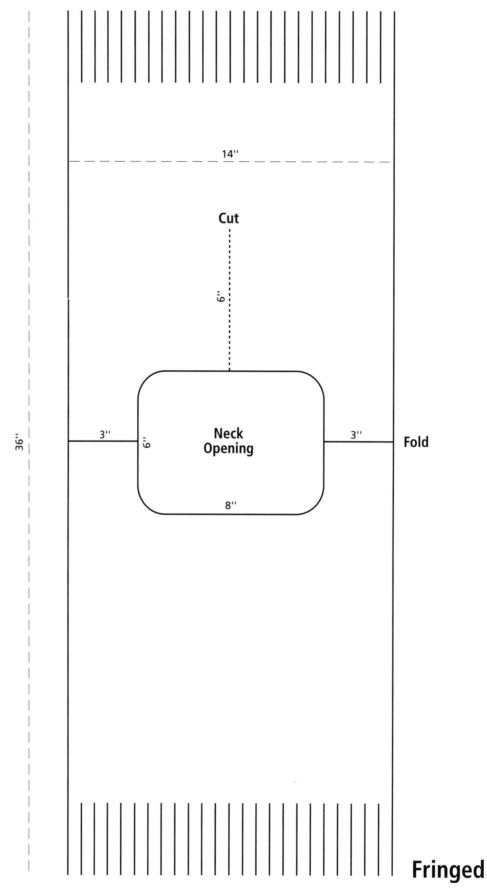

14''

Cut

6''

36''

3''   6''   **Neck Opening**   3''   **Fold**

8''

Fringed

Pattern is shown in reduced size but labeled with full-size dimensions.

Basic Tunic Pattern

Scale: 1" = 4"
Finished Size: 14" × 36"

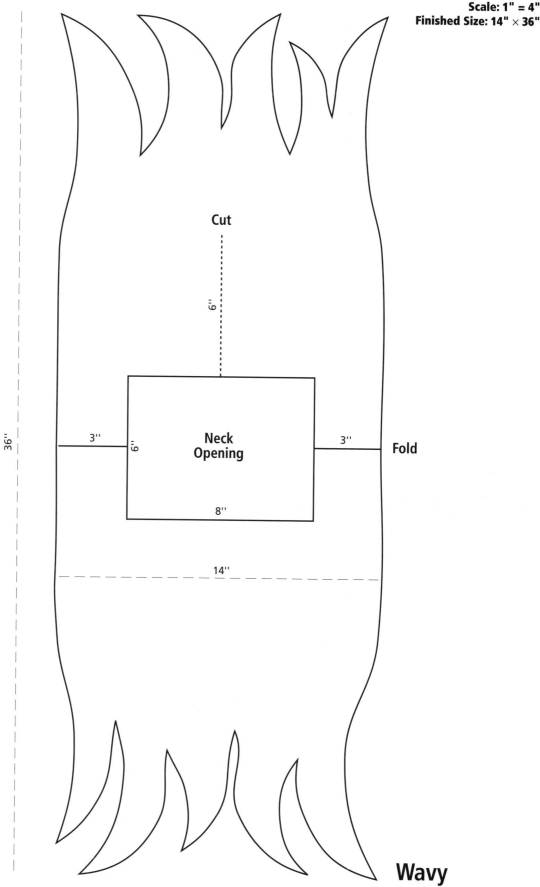

Cut

6"

36"

3"

6"

Neck
Opening

3"

Fold

8"

14"

Wavy

Pattern is shown in reduced size but labeled with full-size dimensions.

Animal Tunic Patterns

Scale: 1" = 5"
Finished Size: 12.5" × 45"

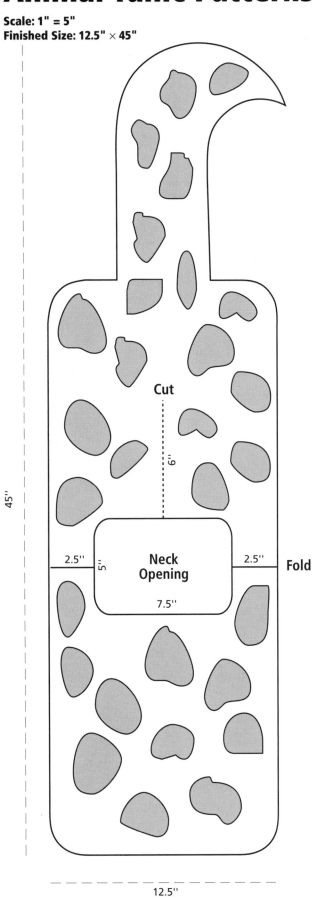

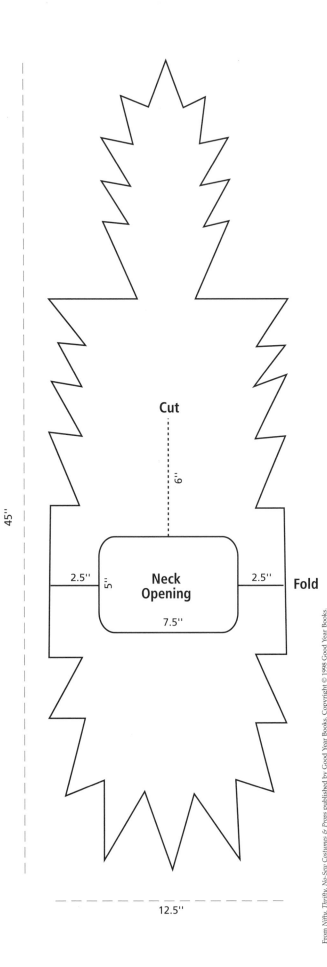

Patterns are shown in reduced size but labeled with full-size dimensions.

From *Nifty, Thrifty, No-Sew Costumes & Props* published by Good Year Books. Copyright © 1998 Good Year Books.

Collar Patterns

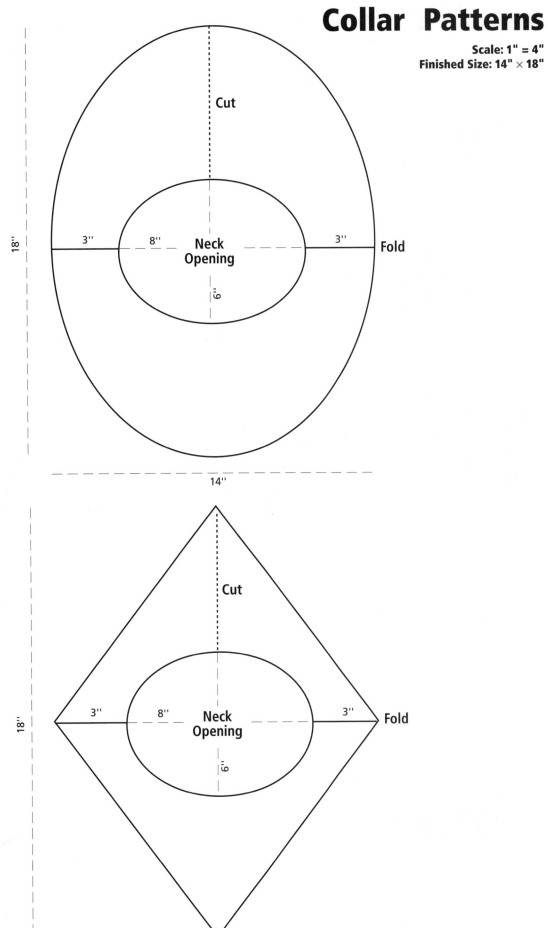

Cut

18"

3''   8''   Neck
Opening   3''   Fold

6''

14''

Cut

18"

3''   8''   Neck
Opening   3''   Fold

6''

From *Nifty, Thrifty, No-Sew Costumes & Props* published by Good Year Books. Copyright © 1998 Good Year Books.

Patterns are shown in
reduced size but labeled
with full-size dimensions.

Collar Patterns

Scale: 1" = 4"
Finished Size: 14" × 18"

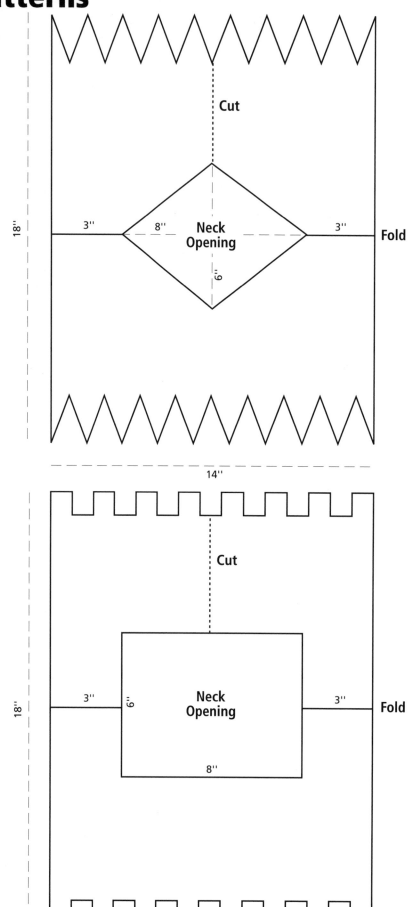

Patterns are shown in
reduced size but labeled with
full-size dimensions.

From *Nifty, Thrifty, No-Sew Costumes & Props* published by Good Year Books. Copyright © 1998 Good Year Books.

Collar Patterns

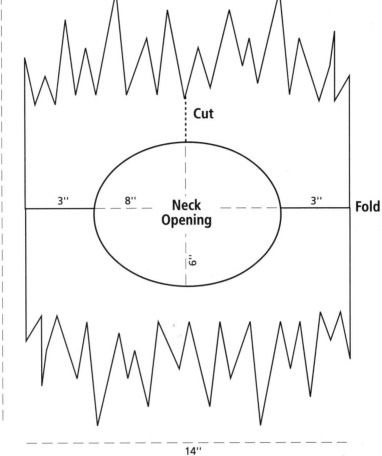

18"

Cut

3"   8"   Neck
Opening   3"   Fold

6"

14"

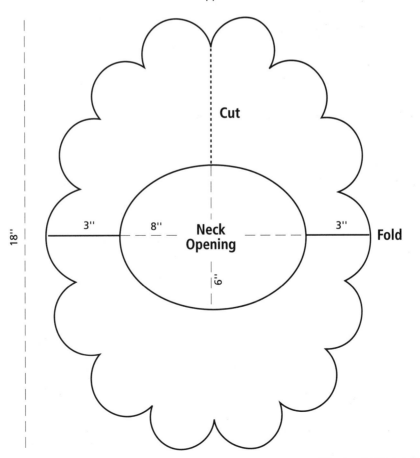

18"

Cut

3"   8"   Neck
Opening   3"   Fold

6"

Patterns are shown in
reduced size but labeled with
full-size dimensions.

Shirt Collar Patterns

Scale: 1" = 1"
Finished Size: 6" × 3"

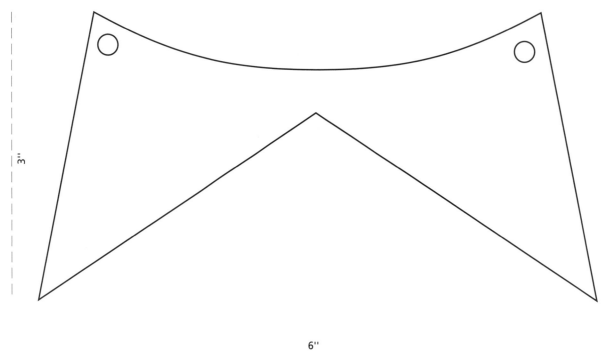

3"

6"

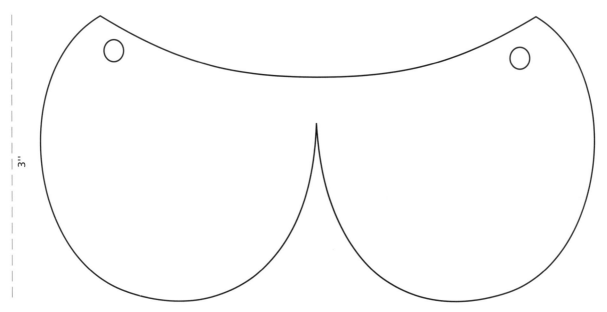

3"

Patterns are shown full-size.

Vest Pattern

Scale: 1" = 3"
Finished Size: 12" × 24"

12"

24"

3"   6"   **Neck Opening**   3"   **Fold**

6"

Pattern is shown in reduced size but labeled with full-size dimensions.

Vest Pattern

Scale: 1" = 3"
Finished Size: 12" × 24"

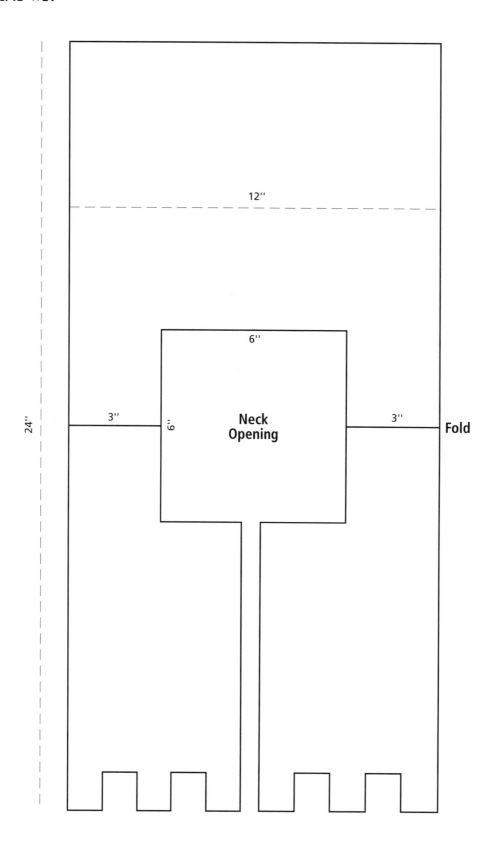

Pattern is shown in reduced size but labeled with full-size dimensions.

Vest Pattern

Scale: 1" = 3"
Finished Size: 12" × 24"

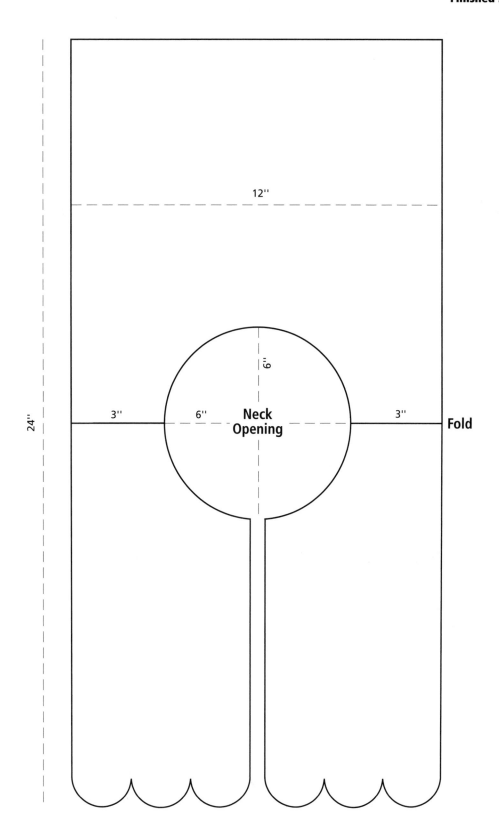

12"

6"

3"   6"   **Neck Opening**   3"   **Fold**

24"

From *Nifty, Thrifty, No-Sew Costumes & Props* published by Good Year Books. Copyright © 1998 Good Year Books.

Pattern is shown in reduced size but labeled with full-size dimensions.

Cape Patterns

Scale: 1" = 6"
Finished Size: 42" × 21"

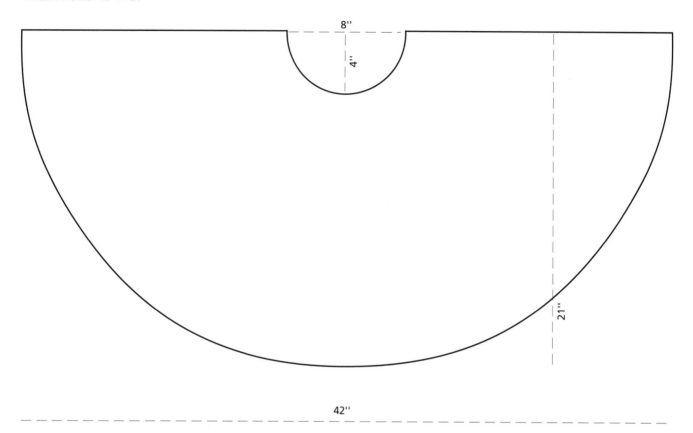

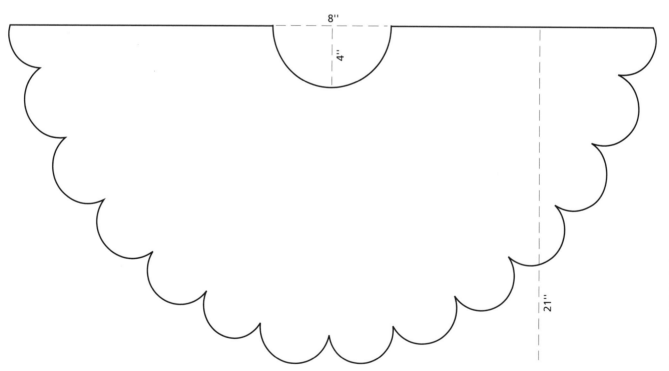

Patterns are shown in reduced size but labeled with full-size dimensions.

Cape Patterns

Scale: 1" = 6"
Finished Size: 42" × 21"

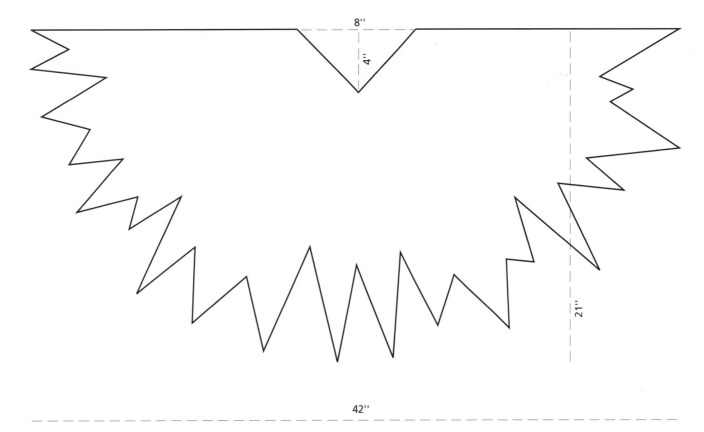

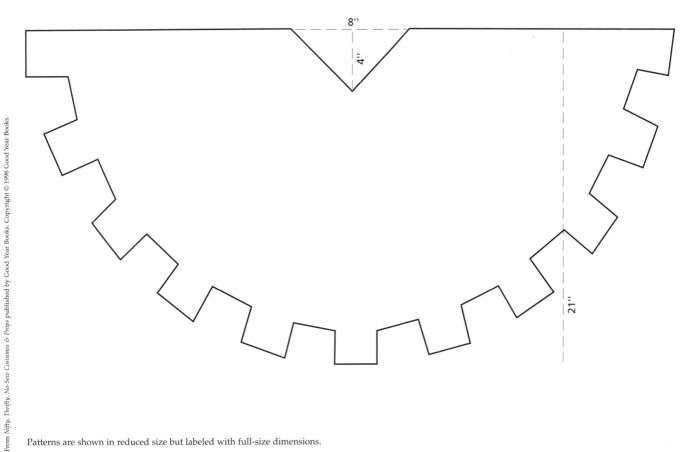

Patterns are shown in reduced size but labeled with full-size dimensions.

Cape Patterns

Scale: 1" = 6"
Finished Size: 42" × 21"

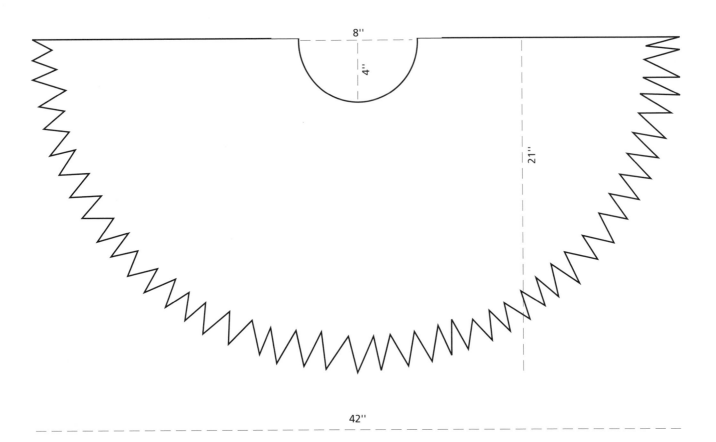

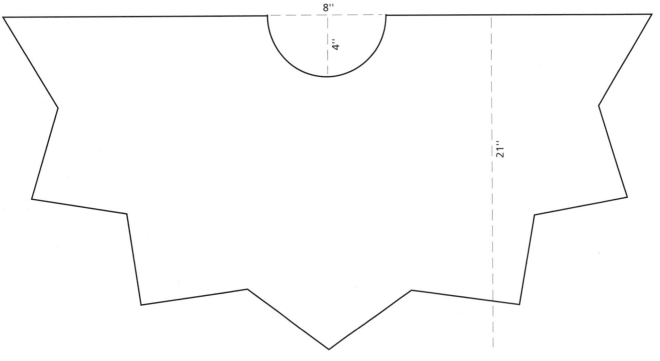

Patterns are shown in reduced size but labeled with full-size dimensions.

Cape Patterns

Scale: 1" = 6"
Finished Size: 42" × 21"

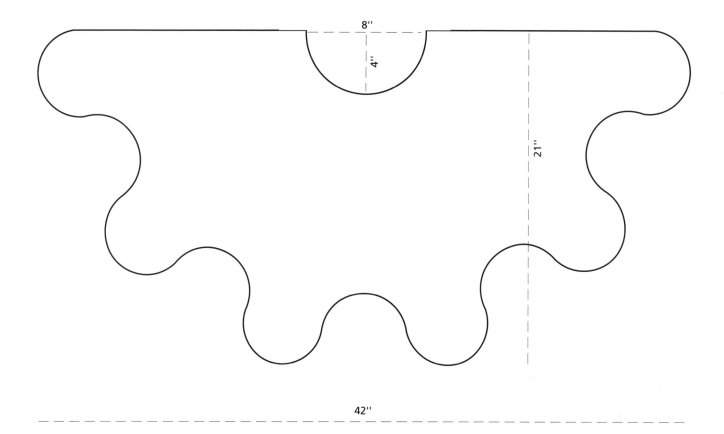

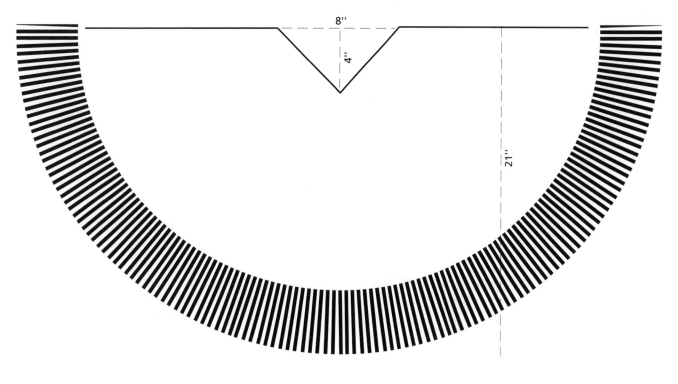

Patterns are shown in reduced size but labeled with full-size dimensions.

Felt Band Hat Pattern

Lengthen the two ends to make a 20"–24" length.

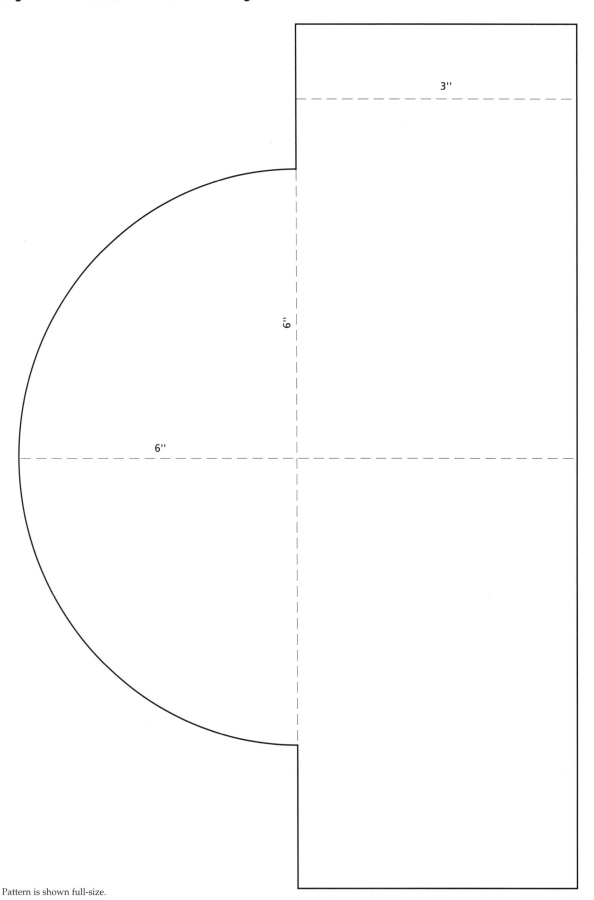

3"

6"

6"

Pattern is shown full-size.

Basic Visor Hat Pattern

Scale: 1" = 1"
Finished Size: 6" × 7"

6''

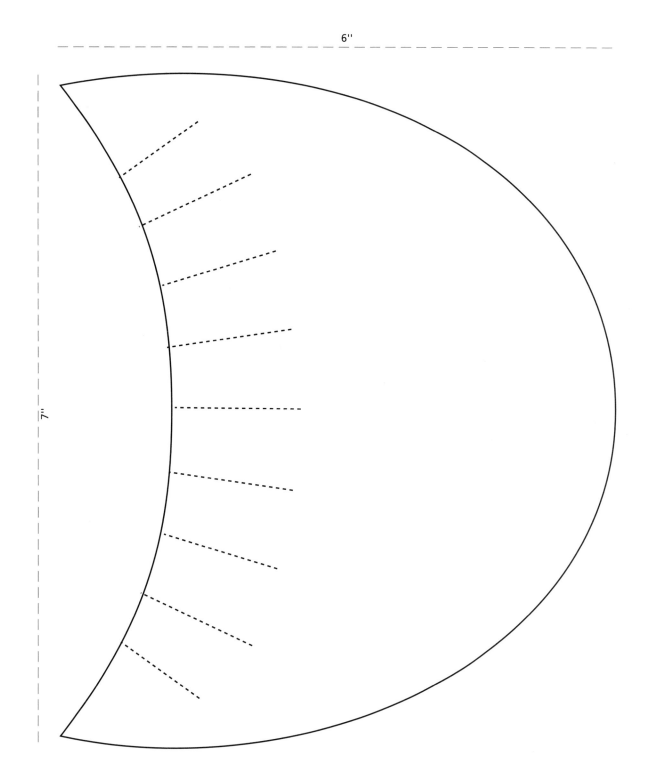

7"

Pattern is shown full-size.

Pirate Hat Pattern

Scale: 1" = 1"
**Fold two 17.5" pieces of poster board
in half, and then use the pattern
to cut out each panel of the hat.**

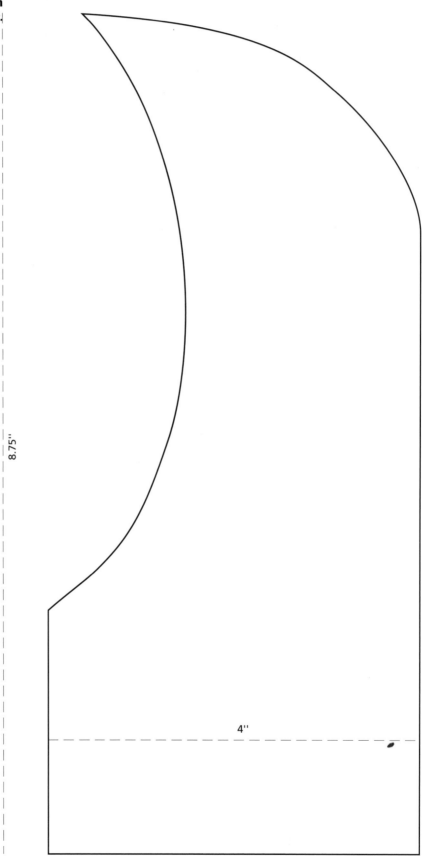

8.75"

4"

Fold

Pattern is shown full-size.

Crown Patterns

Lengthen to 20"–24" long, using same pattern all the way or making the ends plain to become a Tiara.

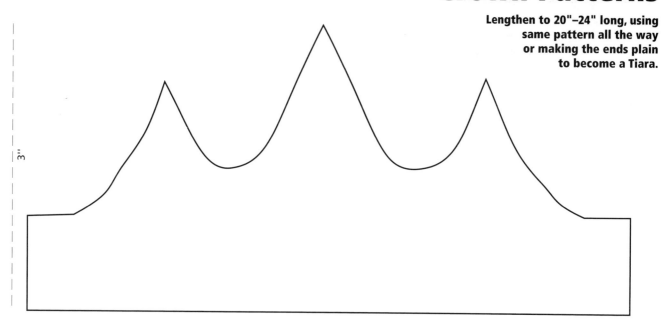

3"

6.5"

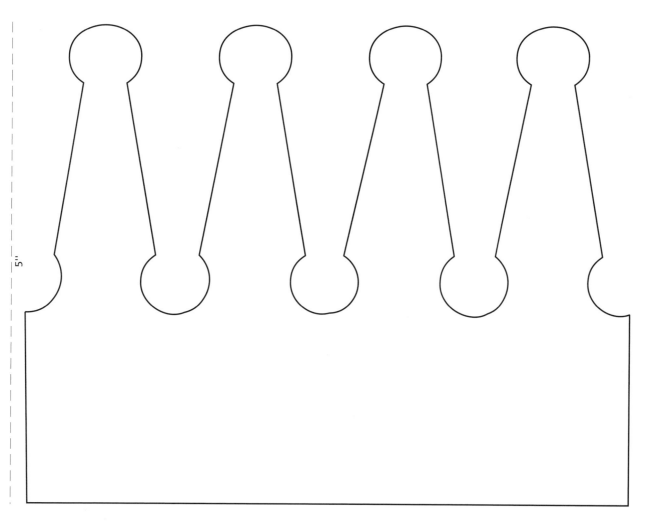

5"

Patterns are shown full-size.

Wing Patterns

Scale: 1" = 3"
Finished Size: Top Pattern 18" × 15"
Bottom Pattern 18" × 9"

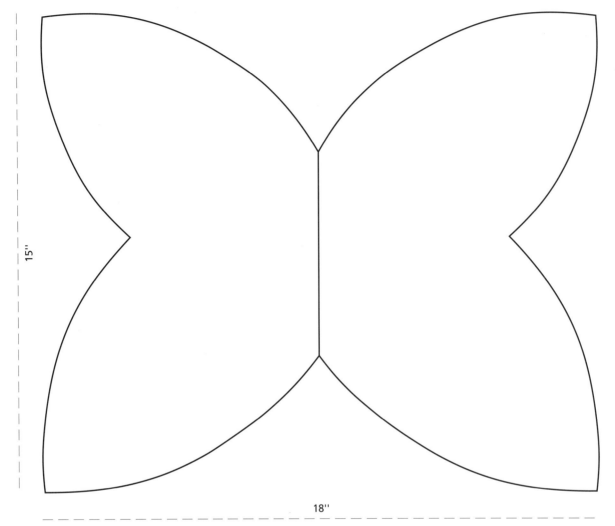

15"

18''

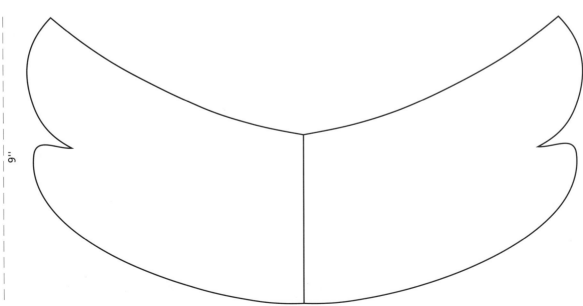

9''

Patterns are shown in reduced size but labeled with full-size dimensions.

Wing Patterns

Scale: 1" = 3"
Finished Size: Top Pattern 18" × 15"
Bottom Pattern 18" × 9"

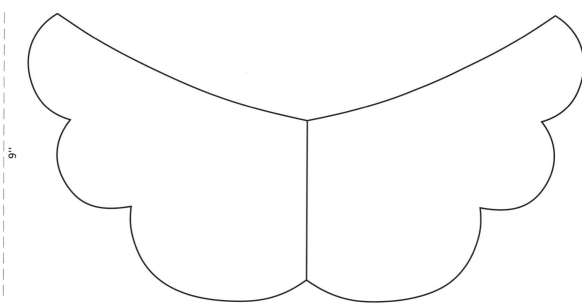

15"

18''

9"

Patterns are shown in reduced size but labeled with full-size dimensions.

Wing Patterns

Scale: 1" = 3"
Finished Size: Top Pattern 18" × 15"
          Bottom Pattern 18" × 9"

15"

18''

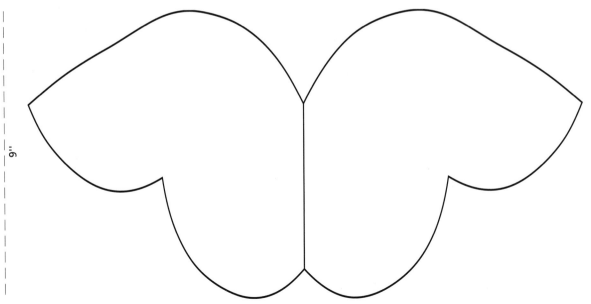

9"

Patterns are shown in reduced size but labeled with full-size dimensions.

From *Nifty, Thrifty, No-Sew Costumes & Props* published by Good Year Books. Copyright © 1998 Good Year Books.

Wing Patterns

Scale: 1" = 3"
Finished Size: Top Pattern 18" × 15"
Bottom Patttern 18" × 9"

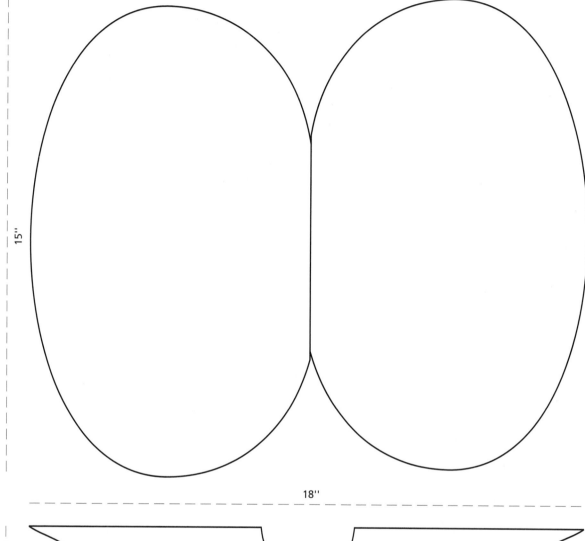

15"

18''

9"

Patterns are shown in reduced size but labeled with full-size dimensions.

CHAPTER

11

Full-Color
Costume and Prop
Reference Guide

This color, alphabetical reference guide depicts 32 finished costumes with a list of pieces and page references so that instructions can be easily found within this book. Simply refer to the page number listed for each piece of the costume to find the full instructions and materials list.

When viewing this section, you can choose to
- make the exact costume depicted or
- vary a costume to create other characters.

(For example, with a few alterations, the Doctor can become a Nurse, the Goat can become a Deer.) All materials selected to construct the costumes are simple and inexpensive, such as felt, glue, fabric paint, yarn. And remember, there is no sewing involved!

From *Nifty, Thrifty, No-Sew Costumes & Props* published by Good Year Books. Copyright © 1998 Good Year Books.

Astronaut

Costume	White Tunic	18
Bottom Cut	Scalloped Pattern	150
Collar, Vest, Cape	Blue Tie-on Collar	22
Decorations, Emblems	Fabric Paint Badge	112
Accessories	Helmet	50
	Felt Boot Tops	74
not shown	Shoe Box Boots	71
Props	Felt Pouch	123
not shown	Tools	130
	Binoculars	124
	Power Beam	126
	Flashlight *(see Police Officer)*	

Ballerina

Costume	Pink Tulle Skirt	28
Accessories	Tulle Hair Pompom with Ribbon	103
	Sock Ballet Slippers	77
not shown here	Tiara *(see Fairy Princess)*	
Props *not shown here*	Assorted Jewelry	104

Bear

Costume	Straight Tan Tunic and Brown Tunic with Fringe	18
Bottom Cut	Straight Cut and Full Rounded Patterns	148
Accessories	Paper Cup Nose with Whiskers	59
	Headband Felt Ears	61
	Felt Paws and Claws	79
not shown here Sock Tail		85

Bird

Costume	Yellow Tunic	18
Bottom Cut	Jagged Pattern	149
Decorations, Emblems	Assorted Feathers Glued to Tunic, Wings, Feet, and Hat *(store bought shown)*	103
Accessories	Bird Hat with Beak	37
	Bird Leg Socks	77
	Felt Bird Feet	79
	Yarn-laced Wings	113
not visable here Felt Tail with Feathers		83

Bumblebee

Costume	Black Tunic	18
Bottom Cut	Straight Pattern	143
Decorations, Emblems	Yellow Felt Stripes	
Accessories	Insect Band	96
	Antennas	89
	Poster Board/Tulle Wings	115

Cat

Costume	White Tunic	18
Bottom Cut	Scalloped Pattern	150
Collar, Vest, Cape	Tie-on Collar	22
Decorations, Emblems	Bow and Bells on Collar	
Accessories	Headband Felt Ears	61
	Paper Cup Nose with Whiskers	59
	Felt Paws and Claws	79
	Sock Tail	85

Cheerleader

Costume	Red and White Crepe Paper Streamer Skirt	28
Collar, Vest, Cape	White Collar	22
Decorations, Emblems	Felt "A" Emblem and Shoulder Decorations	
Accessories	Felt Shoe Tops with Laces	77
Props	Pennant	128
	Cheerleading Pompoms	128
not shown	Megaphone	128

Construction Worker

Costume	Orange Vest	23
Decorations, Emblems	Black Electrical Tape, Felt Pieces	
not shown here	Name Tag	112
Accessories	Construction Hardhat	51
	Felt Boot Tops	74
	Tool Belt	130
Props	Tools	130
	Construction Cone	130
not shown here	Hose *(see Firefighter)*	
	Flashlight *(see Police Officer)*	
	Power Beam	126

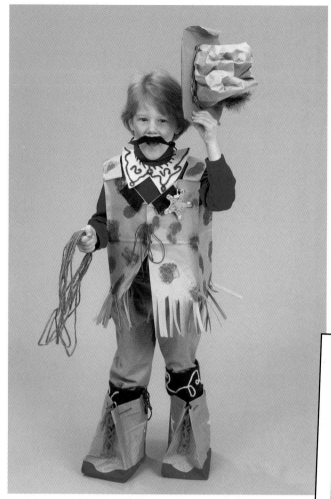

Cowboy

Costume	Brown Paper Bag Vest	24
Bottom Cut	Fringe Pattern	152
Collar, Vest, Cape	Tie-on Collar	22
Decorations, Emblems	Foil-covered Cardboard Star	
Accessories	Paper Bag Western Hat	45
	Mustache	67
	Paper Bag Boots	73
	Felt Boot Tops	74
Props	Rope	134
not shown here	Pouch (*see King*)	

Dinosaur

Costume	Green Tunic	24
Bottom Cut	Scalloped Pattern	150
Collar, Vest, Cape	Green Collar	22
Decorations, Emblems	Felt Scales	
Accessories	Felt Band Hat with Face	36
	Shoe Box Feet	71
	Felt Paws with Claws	79
	Sleeve Tail	85

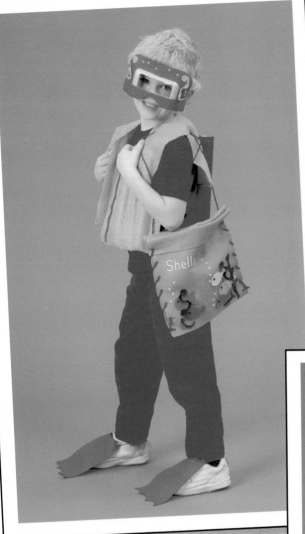

Diver

Costume	Yellow Diver Vest	24
Decorations, Emblems	Fabric Paint, Felt Shapes, Yarn for Lacing	
not shown here	Badge	112
Accessories	Diver Fins	77
	Diver Mask	125
Props	Oxygen Tanks	116
	Felt Tote	123
not shown	Power Beam	126

Doctor

Costume	White Tunic	18
Bottom Cut	Straight Cut Pattern	148
Decorations, Emblems	Felt Red Cross Emblem (Badge)	112
	Name Tag	112
	Felt Pocket	119
Accessories	Examination Hat	34
	Felt Shoe Tops with Laces	77
	Belt	100
	Eyeglasses	125
not shown here	Necktie	101
Props	Doctor Bag (Felt Tote)	123

Dog

Costume	White Tunic with Tail	20
Bottom Cut	Straight Cut Pattern	148
Collar, Vest, Cape	Dog Collar and Tag	100
Decorations, Emblems	Black Felt Spots	
Accessories	Headband Felt Ears	61
	Felt Paws	79

Elf

Costume	Green Tunic	18
Bottom Cut	V-Shaped Pattern	147
Collar, Vest, Cape	Green Collar	22
Decorations, Emblems	Feathers for Hat *(store bought shown)*	103
Accessories	Point Hat	37
	Felt Boot Tops	74
	Belt	100
Props	Felt Pouch	123
	Magic Wand	134

Fairy

Costume	White Tunic	18
Bottom Cut	Scalloped Pattern	150
Collar, Vest, Cape	Collars	22
Decorations, Emblems	Plastic Jewels, Glitter or Liquid Stars (soft fabric paint), Ribbons	
Accessories	Bubble Wrap Skirt	29
	Tiara	51
	Sock Shoes	77
	Poster Board Band Bracelets	109
	Tulle Wings	113
Props	Magic Wand	134

Farmer

Costume	Light Blue Tunic (Overall Straps Added)	18
Bottom Cut	Straight Pattern	148
Decorations, Emblems	Felt Pocket	119
	Fabric Paint, Buttons	
Accessories	Farmer Hat	45
	Felt Boot Tops	74
Props	Basket	124
	Gardening Tools	130
	Eggs Cut from Polystyrene Foam	

Firefighter

Costume		
	Red and Black Collar	22
not shown here	Red Tunic	18
Decorations, Emblems	Badges	112
	Name Tag	113
	Black Electrical Tape	
Accessories	Fire Hat	40
	Felt Boot Tops	74
not shown here	Felt Shoe Tops	77
	Belt	100
Props	Hose	130
not shown	Power Beam	126
	Flashlight (*see Police Officer*)	

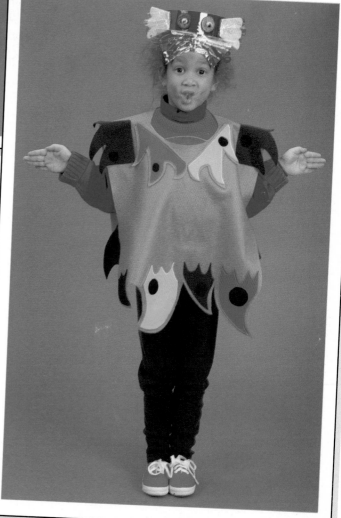

Fish

Costume		
Costume	Light Blue Tunic	18
Bottom Cut	Wavy Pattern	153
Decorations, Emblems	Felt "Scales," Glued-on Squiggle Eyes, Cellophane	
Accessories	Fins Forehead Band	94
not shown	Felt Tail Fin	83

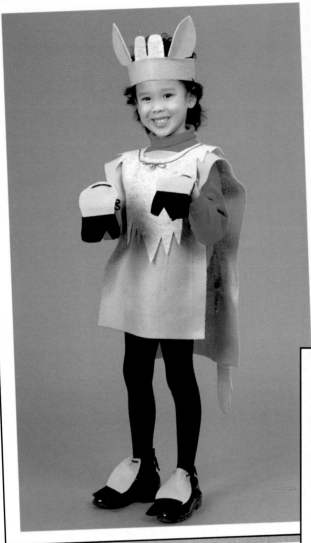

Goat

Costume	Gray Tunic	18
Bottom Cut	Straight Cut Pattern	148
Collar, Vest, Cape	Gray Collar	22
Decorations, Emblems	Bow and Bells Around Neck	
Accessories	Band Hat with Ears and Horns	91
	Felt Hoof Hand and Foot Coverings	79
	Felt Tail	83

Horse

Costume	Tan Tunic	18
Bottom Cut	Straight Cut Pattern	148
Collar, Vest, Cape	Brown Tie-on Collar	22
Decorations, Emblems	Felt Fringed to Resemble Fur	
Accessories	Horse Mane Headband with Ears	61
	Felt Hoof Hand and Foot Coverings	79
	Felt Tail	83

From *Nifty, Thrifty, No-Sew Costumes & Props* published by Good Year Books. Copyright © 1998 Good Year Books.

King

Costume	Purple Tunic	18
Bottom Cut	Straight Cut Pattern	148
Collar, Vest, Cape	Collar (Square-cut)	22
	Red Cape	25
Decorations, Emblems	Plastic Jewels, Fabric Paint for Gold Trim, Foil, Sequins, Ribbon, Liquid Confetti (soft fabric paint), Glitter	
Accessories	Crown	51
	Felt Boot Tops	74
	Felt Shoe Tops with Buckles	77
	Belt	100
	Foil Collar/Necklace	105
Props	Pouch	123
	Scepter	133

Knight

Costume	Gray Tunic	18
Bottom Cut	Squared Pattern	151
Collar, Vest, Cape	Gray Collar	22
Decorations, Emblems	Yarn Trim, Plastic Jewels	
Accessories	Helmet	50
	Felt Boot Tops	74
	Foam Medallion	108
not shown here	Felt Shoe Tops *(see King)*	
	Belt	100
Props	Shield	133
	Sword	133

Mail Carrier

Costume	Dark Blue Tunic	18
Bottom Cut	Straight Cut Pattern	148
Collar, Vest, Cape	Light Blue Shirt Collar	22
Decorations, Emblems	Fabric Paint, Felt Pieces, Buttons	
not shown here	Badges and Name Tag	112
Accessories	Visor Hat	39
	Belt	100
not shown here	Felt Boot Tops	74
	Felt Shoe Tops	77
Props	Mail Bag (Felt Tote)	123

Mermaid

Costume	Dark Green Tunic, Extra Long	18
Bottom Cut	Wavy Pattern	153
Decorations, Emblems	Felt Fins and Shells, Yarn	
Accessories	Headband Hair, Curly	66
	Braid	66
	Hair Bow	102
	Sparkle Clay Necklace	108
	Poster Board Band Bracelet	109
Props *not shown here*	Wand *(see Wizard)*	134

Monster

Costume	Black Tunic	18
Bottom Cut	V-shaped Pattern	147
Collar, Vest, Cape	Tie-on Collar (cut and fringed)	22
Accessories	Eye Band	55
	with Horns	93
	Furry Paws	81

Pirate

Costume	Red Tunic	18
Bottom Cut	Straight Cut Pattern	148
Collar, Vest, Cape	Collar (cut pointed)	22
Decorations, Emblems	Felt Pirate Symbol, Fabric Paint	
Accessories	Pirate Hat	40
	Felt Boot Tops	74
	Belt	100
	Eye Patch	101
not shown here	Felt Shoe Tops	77
	Earring	104
Props	Felt Pouch	123
	Spyglass	124
not shown here	Sword *(see Knight)*	
	Coins	124

Police Officer

Costume	Dark Blue Tunic	18
Bottom Cut	Straight Cut Pattern	148
Collar, Vest, Cape	Blue Shirt Collar	22
Decorations, Emblems	Name Tag	112
	Emblems	112
	Buttons	
Accessories	Visor Hat	39
	Belt	100
	Felt Boot Tops	74
Props	Keys	121
	Flashlight	126
not shown here	License Plate	121
	Driver's License	121
	Wallet	123
	Power Beam	126

Queen

Costume	Maroon Tunic	18
Bottom Cut	Straight Cut Pattern	148
Collar, Vest, Cape	Purple Cape	25
Decorations, Emblems	Fabric Paint, Plastic Jewels, Ribbons, Glitter or Liquid Stars (soft fabric paint)	
Accessories	Crown	51
	Fancy Hands	80
	Foil Necklaces	105
	Felt Pouch	123
Props	Scepter	133

From *Nifty, Thrifty, No-Sew Costumes & Props* published by Good Year Books. Copyright © 1998 Good Year Books.

Restaurant Worker

Costume	White Tunic	18
Bottom Cut	Scalloped Pattern	150
Collar, Vest, Cape	Tie-on Collar	22
Decorations, Emblems	Name Tag	112
	Felt Pocket	119
	Felt Pieces	
Accessories	Felt Band Hat	36
	Kitchen Apron	126
Props *not shown here*	Menus	126
	Baking Pans	126
	Pump Dispenser	127
	Kitchen Utensils	127

Space Alien/Robot

Costume	Gray Tunic	18
Bottom Cut	Straight Cut Pattern	148
Collar, Vest, Cape	Gray Collar	22
Decorations, Emblems	Felt Pieces, Brad Fasteners, Velcro on Collar's Detachable Radio	
Accessories	Band Hat	34
	with Antennae	89
	Felt Boot Tops	74
	Robot Belt	100
	Paper Towel Tube Necklace	105
Props *not shown here*	Flashlight	126
	Power Beam	126
	Spyglass (*see Pirate*)	
	Sword (*see Knight*)	

Tiger

Costume	Orange Tunic	18
Bottom Cut	Jagged Pattern	149
Collar, Vest, Cape	Striped Pointed Collar	22
Decorations, Emblems	Fabric Paint	
Accessories	Plastic Ring Eyes with Nose, Whiskers	57
	Headband Felt Ears	61
	Felt Paws with Claws	79
	Sleeve Tail	85

Wizard

Costume	Purple Tunic	18
Bottom Cut	Straight Cut Pattern	148
Collar, Vest, Cape	Black Cape	25
Decorations, Emblems	Fabric Paint, Glitter or Liquid Confetti (soft fabric paint)	
Accessories	Wizard Cone Hat	41
not shown here	Medallion *(see Knight)* Felt Boot Tops and Shoe Tops *(see King)*	
Props	Crystal Ball	134
	Wizard Wand	134

From *Nifty, Thrifty, No-Sew Costumes & Props* published by Good Year Books. Copyright © 1998 Good Year Books.